The Peak and Pennines

Books on the Peak and Pennines by the same Author

PEAK PANORAMA

THE BACKBONE OF ENGLAND

Companions to this volume

THE LAKELAND PEAKS

THE WELSH PEAKS

THE SCOTTISH PEAKS

Plate 1 **Route 29**—Kinder Downfall in winter

W. A. Poucher, Hon. F.R.P.S.

The Peak and Pennines

from Dovedale to Hadrian's Wall
A pictorial guide to walking in the region
and to the safe ascent of its hills and moors

with 250 photographs by the author
26 maps and 59 routes

Fifth edition

Constable London

First published in Great Britain 1966
by Constable and Company Ltd
10 Orange Street London WC2H 7EG
Copyright © 1966 William Arthur Poucher
Second edition 1973
Third editionm 1978
Fourth edition 1983
Fifth edition 1988

ISBN 0 09 468540 1

Set in Monophoto Times New Roman 9pt
Filmset and printed in Great Britain by
BAS Printers Limited, Over Wallop, Hampshire

Preface to the fifth edition

Since the fourth edition of this work appeared in 1983, my
father has found that increasing age (he is now ninety-six) has
made it impossible for him to undertake any revision necessary
for this new edition and has passed the task to me. In this
regard, I should like to emphasise a request my father always
made:

> 'In view of the vast scope of this book it is obviously
> impossible to check frequently every one of the descriptions
> of the routes. Time, usage, rock falls and local weather may
> be responsible for slight variations, and should any wayfarer
> encounter any inaccuracy I would appreciate a note for
> inclusion in future editions of this work.'

This book, together with its three predecessors devoted
respectively to English Lakeland, Wales and Scotland,
completes a survey of the mountainous country of Britain. But
the situation of the Backbone of England, dealt with in the
present work, is very different from the others in that much of
it lies on the doorstep, so to speak, of many of our great
industrial cities and large towns, and in consequence not only
is access shorter, quicker and easier, but it also allows the keen
climber to reach any near outcrop for an afternoon's sport.
You have only to visit places like Stanage, the Roaches or
Laddow on a fine weekend to see several ropes festooning the
crags. And while this facility of access applies also to the lofty
moors and gritstone outcrops of Kinder, it is perhaps
surprising to find parties of climbers on summits such as
Ingleborough, which is by no means so easily reached. On the
other hand, remoter peaks like Cross Fell seem deserted and
it is a rare experience to encounter another climber on its
dominating summit. The reason for this seeming neglect may

be due to the absence of rock outcrops, which, in fact, are the most powerful magnet to draw the climber.

The wild and desolate moors dappling this vast area are the delight of the rambler, as also the many potholes which are the strict preserve of the speleologist, and through this diverse array of fine scenery runs the sinuous route of the Pennine Way. Through the courtesy of the Ramblers' Association my father was able to include a short summary of its complex windings, and in some of the 59 Routes which follow he has drawn attention to its many interesting features. But some of the hills and moors are not only strictly preserved but on occasion closed to the public during the grouse shooting season from 12 August to 10 December. However, noticeboards are placed at most access points and they indicate clearly the days on which the paths are free from restrictions.

In this volume my father has featured the most popular and enchanting dales, and while some of them can only be explored by the pedestrian, the beautiful scenery of the others has for many years attracted the motorist, who, however, must leave his car and walk a short distance to view the interesting features in the vicinity.

My father's photographs illustrating each monograph, together with the maps and his detailed descriptions of the routes and summit panoramas, will, I hope, facilitate the exploration of the Peak and Pennines, and enable readers to enjoy more fully their holidays in this delectable part of Britain. And since most of them now carry a camera, his monograph on mountain photography (page 35) should help them to obtain more pleasing and satisfactory pictures.

My father was often asked what cameras he used and his reply was that, since the availability of 35 mm film, he always used Leicas. Latterly for monochrome he used the M2 with 35 mm, 50 mm and 90 mm lenses in conjunction with Kodak Plus X film. For colour work he used a Leicaflex with 28 mm, 50 mm, 90 mm, 135 mm and 45/90 mm (Zoom) lenses with his favourite Kodachrome 25 film.

The immensity of the Peak District National Park is

surprising: in fact, it covers an area of 542 square miles of which more than half lies in Derbyshire. Decreasing proportions of the remainder come from Staffordshire, Cheshire, South and West Yorkshire and Greater Manchester.

Safety in the whole region covered by this book is of paramount importance and I would therefore urge leaders of school and youth parties in particular not to venture on these hills and moors unless the weather is favourable, and moreover to insist upon everyone wearing boots and proper clothing. By doing so, they will not only reduce the risk of accidents but also avoid the often needless call for Mountain Rescue.

At the end of this book a ROUTE CARD will be found and should be used by all readers embarking upon a long walk over the moors.

It should be noted that many of the routes described and illustrated herein have been frequented over the years without objection, but they do not necessarily constitute a right of way. Should a reader have any doubts, he would be well advised to consult the owner of the land and ask permission to cross it before embarking upon his walk.

The twenty-six maps are reproduced with the permission of John Bartholomew & Son Limited.

JOHN POUCHER
Gate Ghyll, High Brigham
Cockermouth, Cumbria

Contents

Contents

Contents

Introductory notes

The Peak and Pennines together are generally known as the 'Backbone of England.' This descriptive title gives a certain amount of secret satisfaction to those residing in the north, although the southerner might well cavil at it because the lowest vertebra of the backbone only makes its appearance just to the north of Derby. The Weaver Hills mark its commencement and, rising from the Midland plain, are patterned with variegated fields, dotted with prosperous-looking farms, and embellished here and there with fine groups of trees which often crown the rounded summits of these gently swelling hills. To the north the contours of this long mountain range rise gradually to Kinder Scout, and are intersected by many narrow and beautiful valleys which are so well hidden as to be unseen from most of the hilltops in the district. This constitutes the southern section of the Backbone, and as a conglomeration of hills and dales differs much from its northern section, which not only includes the Backbone itself, but also many prominent 'ribs.' These occur as broad sweeping ridges which themselves enclose on the east the heads of some of Yorkshire's most delightful dales. On the west there are no clearly defined 'ribs' directly connected with the main chain, but two of its outliers stand as sentinels which frown upon Lancashire; Pendle Hill dominates Clitheroe, and Bowland Forest overlooks the county town itself.

The most southerly part of the Pennines covers much of Derbyshire, although it does, in fact, encroach upon the very edges of Staffordshire, Cheshire, Yorkshire and even a minute strip of Lancashire. It is familiarly known as the Peak District, though its Moors and Edges, which are dominated by the flattish top of Kinder, scarcely merit the title. On the north of this fine walking country a great industrial belt envelops the shallowest part of the Backbone to join Lancashire with Yorkshire in a welter of factory chimneys.

Fortunately these thin out in the vicinity of Wharfedale, and beyond Ilkley the lovely undulating hills, often capped by rounded summits, mark the continuation of the range. This country is typical of the moors at their best and is occasionally distinguished by outcrops of rock on its highest contours, but its great charm lies in its glorious woods, sometimes canopying the roads, but more frequently fringing the rivers, all of which variegate the colouring of the wide sweeping dales.

As a whole this section forms a contrasting prelude to the Craven Highlands which as a wide belt of limestone straddles the Pennines and affords a remarkable transformation of the scene and its topography. The softer hues of the moors are here replaced by the greyish whites of the extensive limestone Clints which penetrate the sparse grass to gleam in the sunlight. This part of the country is also characterised by some of the most striking scenery in the whole range, for such well-known features as Malham Cove, Gordale Scar and Kilnsey Crag have to be seen to be believed. Moreover, this region is dominated by Ingleborough, Whernside and Penyghent, three prominent and shapely mountains whose summits are conspicuous objects in the long skyline revealed to advantage from the distant Lakeland Fells. Nor is this all, for the limestone is riddled with potholes whose cavernous recesses carry the mountain streams underground and provide the speleologist with endless material for geological research.

To the north of this belt the rising peaty moorlands become prominent and stretch away through vast solitudes which in places are so remote as to be reminiscent of the distant Cairngorms. The contours fall slightly above Bowes Moor, but beyond it the ground swells up again in a great lonely plateau to culminate in Cross Fell, the highest peak in the Pennines and situated in the north-east corner of Cumbria. The delectable valley of the Tees penetrates these hills on the east and is one of the choicest assets of the County of Durham, but to the north they sink down gradually to Hadrian's Wall and merge ultimately with the desolate lowlands of Scotland.

The Hills

From the brief foregoing description the reader may well ask
how the Pennine country compares with the other
mountainous regions of Britain. Generally speaking the chief
glory of the Pennines is in the broad sweeping lines of its
moors and hills, and while it has a special attractiveness of its
own, there is no doubt that it does not display the splendour
of English Lakeland, the wild grandeur of the Scottish
Highlands, the fretted skyline or soaring Gothic spires of the
Coolins, or the sombre landscape of Snowdonia. Nor does it
possess those spectacular ridges which are the delight of the
mountaineer, such as Striding Edge on Helvellyn, Aonach
Eagach the north wall of Glencoe, or the famous Horseshoe
of North Wales. There are, however, many modest but
shapely hills, and here Penyghent scores over the rest of the
Pennine giants with its southern escarpment disclosing some
fine outcrops of gritstone which impart a distinctive character
to the mountain. There may be some who will dispute its pre-
eminence and prefer to give the palm to Ingleborough, but
aside from its striking aspect when seen from Chapel-le-Dale,
Ingleborough's top appears as a mere hump in the high
sprawling plateau. In the same way the proximity of the
adjacent high moorland detracts from the impressiveness of
Cross fell, which is the highest peak in the whole chain,
Mickle Fell, further to the south, suffers from similar
disadvantages, as does Great Whernside also, the massive hill
above Kettlewell in Wharfedale. It is strange that this
Yorkshire giant should have a more important title than its
namesake further to the west, but this may be due to its bulk
alone, because the latter is nearly 100 feet higher and
decidedly more shapely. Baugh Fell and Wild Boar Fell have
a fine elevation when seen from the vicinity of Garsdale
Junction, and when the mist swirls round Nine Standards
Rigg, it too can assume dramatic proportions from the low
hills above Kirkby Stephen.

The hills of the Peak District are perhaps less striking because the whole area is fairly high, but Lose Hill and Win Hill have a singular charm when seen from certain angles, while the most impressive aspect of Kinder Scout is from the west when the great semicircle of gritstone precipices enclosing the Downfall looks gigantic from the hills near Hayfield Reservoir. The southern and eastern sections, however, are characterised by many fine gritstone outcrops and Edges, that are unique in our British scenery. Like the long broken battlements of an old fortress, they perhaps look their best in the setting sun, when their innumerable splintered facets reflect the evening glow and sparkle like rows of jewels strung across the lofty landscape. Stanage Edge is about four miles long and probably the most beautiful of them all. Here the high moorland plateau suddenly ends and a line of supporting precipitous gritstone cliffs, up to 100 feet in height, separates it from the first declivities of the valley which sink down gently to the woods fringing the river that threads its floor. To revel in the long walk along this Edge you should traverse its full length northwards in the evening while the sun goes down in a blaze of glory; you will then indeed have experienced one of the major delights of the whole district.

Gritstone is a joy to the rock climber and most of the Edges have been fully explored by the many devotees of this sport. To appreciate the grip this stone can give the feet, you should climb up to Robin Hood's Cave. There is nothing else like it. Stanage Edge is, however, only one of the playgrounds of these sportsmen, for every gritstone outcrop is well marked by the boot nails of past enthusiasts (though nowadays they wear vibrams or rock boots which do not damage the delicate holds). Gritstone cliffs are distributed throughout the region and several of them are featured in this book. The favourites are probably Laddow, Stanage, Cromford and Kinder Scout in the Peak, the Roaches in Staffordshire, and Almscliff and Ilkley in Yorkshire. In recent years many of the Quarries have come into favour and typical examples are those of Millstone Edge and Lawrencefield, situated on either side of the Surprise

View, where the nearly vertical routes require free rock climbing of the very high standard. Moreover, while the conspicuous layer of gritstone on Penyghent may be more striking in appearance, it is very shattered but has now received the attention of a number of climbers. Forty years ago climbing on the Limestone Outcrops was frowned upon as too dangerous for safety, whereas today tough experts successfully tackle those at Stoney Middleton, Water-cum-Jolly and the spectacular tors in Dovedale and Chee Dale in the Peak, while Malham Cove, Gordale Scar and Kilnsey Crag in the Pennines have also been thoroughly explored.

Those who love moorland walking will find the Pennines much to their taste. It is true enough that in Derbyshire many of the moors are sometimes inaccessible because they are preserved for grouse, but in spite of the innumerable notice boards warning off the trespasser, people do roam about them in the off season as I did to secure the photographs for this book. Some of the moors are protected by fences which approximate in height to the deer fences in the Highlands, and it would be a ticklish job to cross those enclosing Bamford Edge, a fine gritstone escarpment frowning upon the Derwent Reservoir. The northern section of the Pennines, however, does not appear to suffer so much from these disadvantages and those who wish to seek solitude in the high places will find it easily on the Mickle Fell–Cross Fell group of hills. Here the lofty moorland stretches as far as the eye can see and you have to keep a wary glance for the bogs which abound everywhere. It is a good pull to attain the highest part of this great ridge, let alone to walk its full length. You may see a few sheep, but your companions will be the cloud and wind, the plover and the curlew. The peak-bagger will have a happy time in the Pennines because there are so many summits, and, unlike the Lakeland Fells, they are separated by great distances. The views from them are spacious and often repaying; one of the best is from Ingleborough, where to the west you look to the serrated skyline of the blue Lakeland hills, and to the east to the seamed façade of Penyghent.

The Craven Highlands are famous for their topography, for aside from the spectacular features of Malham Cove, Gordale Scar and Kilnsey Crag, the whole of this limestone belt is riddled with pot-holes. They are dangerous places near which to loiter, especially on a misty day, but are nevertheless well worthy of inspection from the adjacent moorland. Gaping Gill is the most notorious, and it requires a steady head to stand on the verge of the hole and to look down onto the blue haze which masks its fearsome depth. Alum Pot is more charmingly situated, for it is surrounded by trees, but the gash itself is awesome, and when you look down and your eyes get accustomed to the gloom you will be able to pick out the ferns which grow in profusion on its sheer walls. All the pot-holes have been explored and here the speleologist is in his element. He may descend the main shaft in a bosun's chair, or descend by abseil on a long rope. This is, however, only an introduction to the game, for he then follows the subterranean passages and chambers, swimming through deep pools or fording underground rivers, to delight in the fantastic encrustations, stalactites and stalagmites, all of which glitter mysteriously in the light of his headlamp. In addition to these adventurous attractions, there are beautiful caves near Castleton, Ingleton and Pately Bridge, all of which can be explored with a guide on payment of a small fee.

A glance at the maps of both Peak and Pennines will reveal the wealth of tarns and lakes sprinkled about this long line of hills. Of the small ones, the Mermaid's Pool in the very shadow of Kinder Scout is one of the most charming; when seen from the edge of the cliffs it glitters like a brilliant sapphire on the sombre slopes of this vast peak. Of the larger ones, Malham Tarn and Semer Water occupy the premier positions, but the lack of beauty in their setting detracts considerably from their appeal and they do not compare favourably with the exquisite lakes and larger tarns of English Lakeland or with the superb and colourful lochs of Scotland. A large number of the sheets of water in the Backbone of England are in fact reservoirs, but it must be admitted that the various bodies responsible for their construction have in many cases done their best to improve the new landscape by planting trees to soften the prospect. Good examples of this planning are the three completed reservoirs in the Derwent valley where the trees have matured sufficiently to make the walk along their winding banks a real pleasure.

The Dales

It is in its valleys that the Pennine country is seen at its best. They are not gloomy and impressive like Wasdale, Llanberis or Glencoe, but for sheer beauty are indeed hard to beat. Some of them are narrow defiles, hidden away from the searching gaze of the climber on his hilltop, while others are on the grand scale and wind their way deeply into the fastnessess of the hills. They act as immense catchment areas and the rivers which grace them are some of the most beautiful in Britain. There are also an abundance of waterfalls, with a cascade at almost every bend in the stream, so that when you walk along their banks you have water music all the way. And what can be more enchanting?

Dovedale is pre-eminent among the sinuous narrow defiles of the region. It is hemmed in by striking limestone pinnacles which tower above the masses of lovely trees and look down upon the placid stream which the trout fishermen proclaim as their Utopia. Chee Dale is on a more dramatic scale, and the closing of the railway throughout its entire length has now restored the great charm it formerly possessed. It is one of the most beautiful in the region and should be traversed from east to west if its amazing topography is to be seen at its best.

Wharfedale is the loveliest of the larger valleys. It is the pride of Yorkshire and who will dispute it? Here you find a beautiful river, fringed with noble trees and graced with delightful villages, passing through a sweeping dale enclosed by lofty moors, and all within reach of some of our greatest cities. But if you prefer waterfalls and the tinkling music of leaping cascades, go to Wensleydale, where you will discover them in abundance. Aysgarth Falls are famous and strangely enough many tourists are content to merely see the upper fall from the bridge, whereas the middle and lower falls are infinitely superior, but are seen only by those who care to walk through the woods and descend to the rocky bed of the river. Hardrow Force near Hawes is unique and easily accessible, although you must pass through the parlour of a small inn to see it. If you love quiet and beautiful rivers you will one day discover the Lathkill, for it is the most placid and peaceful stream I know, especially the stretch of it below Over Haddon, where you may sit on its green mossy banks and see the trout rising to the surface while the gentle plash of water passing over the weirs makes music like the muted strings of a celestial orchestra.

The Pennine villages are another great attribute, and there is something about them that appeals strongly to romantic folk, for they undoubtedly have a charm and beauty which is difficult to excel elsewhere in this country. There are many who aver that Tissington is the finest of them all; but what about Arncliffe, with its sunny village green and overhanging heights—the gem of Littondale; or Kettlewell, with its chattering beck and quaint old houses and inns—the pride of Wharfedale; or Bainbridge, with its spacious green and shady trees—the delight of Wensleydale; all shining jewels in luxuriant valleys. But even these are perhaps surpassed by West Burton, a model of dainty architecture tucked away in the folds of the hills off Wensleydale. It is the epitome of peace, quietness and contentment. Here you may relax and laze away the hours amid ideal surroundings playing a game of cricket with the laughing children or loitering on the smooth turf of the green to chat with the older inhabitants. If you doubt these lofty tributes look at the pictures in these pages and then go and see the places for yourself. You will perhaps find the village of your dreams to which you may want to retire from the turmoil of the city.

The Weather

Atmospheric conditions play a most important role in the
enjoyment of a holiday in the hills, for while ardent walkers
never mind a good soaking, fine and sunny days with excellent
visibility are always more appreciated. Like all other hill
districts the Peak and Pennines have their quota of rainy
spells, but they are much lower than those in the mountainous
regions bordering the west coast; a fair comparison taken
from *British Rainfall* suggests they are about half. The
connoisseur will immediately say that rain is not the real
hazard in hill country, which is of course true. It is more
particularly the clinging mists that shroud the high ground
and interfere with good visibility that cause trouble, so much
so that any climber who explores the lofty moors, like Kinder
or Bleaklow, in these conditions should make full use of his
map and compass if he is to return to the valley in safety.

The most promising seasons are spring and autumn, and
during April, May and June a blue sky and sailing white
cumulus are not uncommon and add so much to the glory of
this landscape by the glint of light on rock faces, rivers and
trees, to say nothing of the large reservoirs that dapple the
district. To many lovers of the hills this scene of gaiety is not
only equalled but even surpassed by the reds, yellows and
browns of autumn and it is at this time, and particularly in
late October, that the colour photographer secures in sunny
conditions those transparencies that are the delight of every
camera enthusiast.

Conclusion

From this brief résumé it will be apparent to all readers who
love the Peak and Pennines that to climb every hill in the
region, to explore every stretch of moorland, to walk through
every dale, to follow every stream to its source, to visit every
gritstone and limestone outcrop let alone climb their
multitude of courses, and to inspect every cave and pothole
requires at least a long lifetime. But should the reader happen
to reside in one of the towns or cities within easy reach of it,

he will have a better chance of enjoying its varied scenery than the holidaymaker who spends a fortnight, or even a month, roving round the district. Moreover, at the present time most of our young people have ample funds for holidays, and since youth hostelling and camping are an inexpensive form of travel there is no valid reason why they too should not explore and enjoy this splendid countryside. Of course, the almost universal use of the motor car has brought within range many of the beauty spots that a few decades ago would have been difficult of access to all save the tough hiker, but even so the problem of selection arises in which event some indication of where to go and what to see is of inestimable value.

And it is here that this volume should be the guide and friend of all who love this delectable Backbone of England. But in view of its immensity I have been compelled to be severely selective, and in consequence have chosen not only those features that have appealed to me as both interesting and picturesque, but also those that I believe readers of all ages will wish to see for themselves. The inclusion of a wide selection of my photographs will perhaps be more useful than the meagre illustrations in an ordinary guide book; for by consulting this volume in conjunction with my other works devoted to this region they will not only be able to choose their centre with certainty, their routes to the places of interest in the vicinity in accordance with their particular tastes, and the subjects for their cameras if they happen to be photographers, but they will also be able to *see* beforehand through the medium of my camera studies, precisely the type of scenery that will satisfy every one of their needs.

Equipment

Anyone who ventures on the hills and moors without proper equipment is asking for trouble, and since the weather is one of our greatest hazards it is wise, and indeed imperative, to be prepared for sudden and unexpected changes, as for instance from warm sunshine to rain or blizzard, by wearing proper boots and clothing, as well as other relatively inexpensive but useful incidentals which I shall enumerate in these pages.

Boots are of course the most important item and should be of stout construction, not only for the traverse of the lofty moors where peat groughs and damp stretches of bog are common, but also for climbing the gritstone and limestone outcrops which abound in this region. While vibram-soles are in general use for this purpose, most climbers prefer lighter shoes with stiffened soles and pointed toes.

Good climbing boots are expensive, but those who can afford the best will be amply repaid by their comfort and service through years of tough wear. There are several patterns. Light fell boots with good vibram soles are now widely used, some of them with matching and effective gaiters. My own preference is for those in which the leather is in one piece with the joint at the heel and no stitching at the toe, together with padded ankles where most friction occurs. There are advantages and disadvantages in vibrams; they are silent and easier on the feet on *dry* rock, but on *wet* rock or moss-covered slabs they can be a handicap to rapid progress because the utmost care becomes imperative to avoid a slip which in an exposed situation might result in a twisted or broken ankle. Strong laces are vital and are almost universally of nylon or equivalent artificial fibres.

Makers of climbing footwear are always trying to improve upon the normally used type, and the latest to come up with a boot and shoe that promises well is Karrimor. After innumerable experiments a design has been evolved, known as K-SB, that is light weight, waterproof and supple, with a new Klets sole that is non-slip on either grass or rock. Even the elegant shoes are ideal for fell walking and smart enough for casual wear. I have worn a pair of K-SB Trail and found them the most comfortable in my long experience.

Stockings and socks are worthy of some attention and one of each worn together ensure comfort and warmth and reduce undue friction. The *colour* of these items may be important and for some years I have worn *red* ones because in case of accident this colour can be seen at a great distance, and in consequence would facilitate location and subsequent rescue.

Clothes are perhaps a matter of personal taste, and there are still a few climbers who delight in wearing their oldest cast-off suits, often intentionally with brilliant patches as a decoration! But there is more protection when wearing a properly made *Alpine Jacket*, of which there are a variety of patterns and colours, and one of the smartest for summer wear on the hills is a Berghaus Alpen Lovat. They are usually made from closely woven cotton of double texture at the main points of friction. They are windproof and reasonably waterproof and perfectly so if treated with silicone. The better models have four pockets, of which two are large enough to accommodate maps which are then kept dry. A skirt is now made to all types, and in heavy rain keeps moisture from percolating on to the small of the back. The collar could be lined with wool to keep the neck warm in the absence of a scarf. In some of the more expensive models there is a small zip opening below the back of the neck to accommodate the hood when not in use. Outside belts are no longer worn because they may put a rock climber off balance by inadvertently catching on a tiny excrescence of crag. They are now universally replaced by a draw cord which runs in a groove at the waist between the double-texture cloth. This type of Alpine Jacket has a zip fastener down the front and goes well up into the neck, whereas *Anoraks* are made in one piece, with a large kangaroo pocket at breast height and a short zip only at the neck. The most useful of these models have a lower pocket on each side. Nylon is now replacing cotton in some models. For climbers who prefer a smart garment for wear in cold weather on the tops, I have found nothing better than a Pointfive High Sierra Jacket with double open ended zips, which is exceptionally light and warm. In very stormy weather a Gore-Tex Mistral gives the best protection as it keeps out the rain and allows the perspiration to evaporate through the material. In view of the very rapid changes of temperature encountered in hill country, it is always advisable to carry spare *Pullovers*. Those made of light Shetland wool are much better than a heavy one, because the layers of warm air between them maintain the body temperature, and the number worn can be easily adjusted to varying conditions. *Thermal Underwear* close to the skin has reduced the risks of cold, and by its use on the upper and lower body, the weight of necessary insulation. *Leg Gear* is a matter of personal taste; some climbers swear by trousers while others prefer breeches. I have found the latter more comfortable and in addition they allow more freedom about the feet. The *material* from which they are made is another consideration. Many have a preference for corduroy, but I do not care for it because it is made of cotton and therefore cold to the skin, and when it gets very wet the material acts like a sponge and retains an excess of moisture. The weight about the legs then increases and is attended by much discomfort. Alternatively, hardwearing and close-woven tweed is warm and light in weight and altogether more amenable in all mountain weather. *Headgear* has changed considerably in recent years, and the feathered, velour Austrian hat is seldom seen nowadays. The more practical and useful protection is at present confined to two types; the woollen brightly coloured *Bob-Cap* and the old-fashioned *Balaclava Helmet*. In fair weather the former functions admirably and will not blow off in a strong wind, whereas the latter is indispensable in Alpine conditions. In heavy rainfall the best protection is obtained by wearing a proofed nylon smock, the *Cagoule*, which extends down to the knees.

GORE-TEX is a micro porous film which is laminated between the inner and outer layers of fabric and promises to be of great value in mountaineering clothing. For, while the internal body vapour is allowed to escape, the wearer keeps dry and comfortable and at the same time is protected from rain and wind. Recently it has often been used in lightweight bibbed salopettes, especially for winter conditions. Interested readers are respectfully referred to a complete account of it in the 7th edition of my *Lakeland Peaks*.

Rucksacks are a necessity and may be obtained in a variety of shapes, colours, sizes and weights. If the climber is moving from place to place and wishes to carry spare clothing, incidentals and photographic gadgets, then it must be a large one such as a Berhaus or Karrimor or Lowe manufacture, otherwise a small light model should suffice. Some prefer those having a light metal frame which keeps the sack off the back and so allows plenty of ventilation. A leather or cordura base to both sack and side-pockets increases its durability.

Maps of this extensive region should be the guide and friend of all who explore the Backbone of England. There are two series of outstanding merit; and if dissected and mounted on linen they are more easily handled out of doors, but the present cost is so prohibitive that their general use is declining. The 1-inch series issued by the Ordnance Survey referred to in previous editions of this work has been replaced by maps at the scale of 1:50000, the contour intervals of the latest series being at 10 metres. The Tourist Map of the Peak District National Park is a splendid piece of cartography in which the moors and Edges are clearly defined; it extends northwards from Dovedale to Laddow. The 1:50000 series sheet numbers applicable to this book are as follows; Ilkley and Almscliff,

104; Brimham Rocks, 99; Wharfedale, Wensleydale, Swaledale, Malham, Penyghent, Ingleborough and Whernside, 98; Tan Hill, High Force, Caldron Snout, High Cup Nick, Cross Fell and Dufton, 91; Hadrian's Wall, 87. A map of the last named at the scale of 2 inches to a mile indicates every feature of the Wall and its adjacent countryside, and will be an indispensable asset to all who walk the full length of this historic barrier. The Three Peaks map at the scale of 1:25000 will be a welcome addition to all climbers and the Dark Peak map on the same scale will be invaluable to walkers of the Pennine Way as it includes details of Kinder Scout, Bleaklow and Black Hill.

The $\frac{1}{2}$-inch series issued by Bartholomew, now replaced by maps at the scale of 1:100000 have the contours at intervals of 250 feet, but the excellent layer system of colouring reveals the topography of the country with great clarity. The maps in this work are marked with the various routes and should be of immense value to all walkers.

A compass should always be carried in the hills, despite the fact that it may not be needed in clear weather if the ground is familiar. In mist, however, all mountains become wrapped in deeper mystery with the complete disappearance of well-known landmarks, and if the climber is off the beaten track he may well find himself in difficulties without one. Even in clear weather a compass is especially useful on the lofty moors because many of them have tracks that are less distinct than those encountered in Lakeland and Snowdonia. A good compass is not cheap, but it is money well spent. Mountain Photographers should note that certain types of exposure meter containing a magnet may deflect the compass needle if the two are within a short distance of one another. Tests I have made indicate that at a distance of 9 inches N, 12 inches E, and 18 inches S and W the magnetic north is deflected, and when the exposure meter is close to the compass the needle simply spins round. Climbers should therefore test the two instruments and keep one well away from the other when in use, as in misty weather incorrect route finding might result and so lead to unforeseen difficulties.

An aneroid is a most useful instrument and may be a luxury to all save the explorer. A good one is a fairly reliable forecaster of the weather, and since it approximately indicates the altitude it may be a valuable aid in misty weather by helping to locate one's position with greater accuracy. The lower-priced instruments register up to 10,000 feet. If you possess one, always remember to adjust the dial to the altitude of the starting point of your climb, if it is known with certainty, and thereafter check at any known station. Bear in mind that when the barometer is falling the readings will be too high, and if it is rising they will be too low. In any event the error is about 100 feet for each 1/10 of an inch of rise or fall not due to change of altitude.

An ice axe is valuable and may be indispensable in snow climbing; moreover, it is a useful tool for glissading and its correct employment will ensure a safe and rapid descent of steep snow slopes. There are numerous makes, each of which has some slight variation in design of both pick and adze. A competent dealer will advise on the most suitable type, which is largely governed by length of shaft, weight and balance. A sling is a useful adjunct and may prevent the loss of the axe if it should slip out of the hand when in use.

In conclusion, I would advise everyone venturing on the hills at any time of year to carry the following items which could spell survival in extremely bad weather. 1, Map and Compass; 2, Torch and Whistle; 3, Spare Food and Clothing, including a large polythene bag; and 4, a small First Aid Kit.

Rock climbing and hiking

Mountaineering in the generally accepted sense is scarcely applicable to the hills featured in this volume, unless of course severe winter conditions transform peaks like Cross Fell or Ingleborough into giants of Alpine splendour. That this is possible was confirmed by my own experience when I made several solo ascents in the Peak District over snow and ice, including that of Kinder Scout, where sound knowledge and the use of an ice axe proved indispensable to safety.

On the other hand, Rock Climbing is an important sport in this vast region, which is dappled with outcrops of gritstone and limestone, together with many quarries. The fact that these treasured playgrounds are of no great height when compared with the imposing cliffs of Lliwedd in Snowdonia, Scafell in English Lakeland, or Ben Nevis in Scotland, is of little consequence because some of the outcrops like those of the Roaches, Malham, Gordale and Kilnsey, with their spectacular overhangs, call for rock climbing of a very high standard which is only achieved by the really tough expert. Thus, height alone is no criterion of difficulty, and if you are an interested novice you would be well advised to make your first acquaintance of these steep and often vertical walls in the company of an experienced friend.

Should you become keen on this fascinating sport, you may wish to apply for membership of one of the famous clubs, such as the Yorkshire Ramblers or the Rucksack or Wayfarers' Clubs whose standards of admission are high, but like many of those in other mountain regions they may be already full and in consequence you may have to be content with becoming a member of a local but equally experienced organisation. Readers who are interested in this sport should consult *Rock Climbing in the Peak District* (1987 ed.) by Paul

Nunn—a photographic guide in this series of books published by Constable.

Much of the country described and illustrated herein can be explored by the ordinary walker, and pedestrians of all ages should experience no difficulty in ascending any of the peaks included in this volume. Moreover, it is usually quite easy to attain the more lofty Edges, and paths along them, like the four miles on Stanage, afford interesting and enchanting walks. Some of the routes, such as the complete circuit of Kinder, are of considerable length and should only be attempted by those who are in fit condition, whereas the strolls through the charming Dales are relatively short and can be done by anyone. Walkers who are not only interested in the topographical features included in this book, but also in the Pennine Way which threads much of it, may like to join the Ramblers' Association, in which event they should write to the Secretary at 1/5 Wandsworth Road, London SW8 2XX.

Pot-holing is a popular sport in the limestone areas, and readers who are interested should consult the literature devoted especially to speleology, and if keen, join one of the local clubs of which there are many. Some of the more famous pot-holes are noticed in passing, and several Caves open to the public are also mentioned. In any case, no one should enter a Cave alone or attempt to descend any hole in the ground without a competent and experienced companion, otherwise they will be looking for trouble that might well lead to disaster.

Heights of the principal peaks and passes

Arranged in order of altitude, in feet O.D.

1	2,930	Cross Fell	30	2,039	Higher Shelf Stones
2	2,591	Mickle Fell	31	2,023	Tor Mere Top
3	2,415	Whernside	32	2,015	Wether Fell
4	2,372	Ingleborough	33	1,937	Blackden Edge
5	2,340	Great Shunner Fell	34	1,834	Shining Tor
6	2,328	High Seat	35	1,810	Axe Edge
7	2,310	Great Whernside	36	1,082	Rushup Edge
8	2,302	Buckden Pike	37	1,793	Margery Hill
9	2,277	Penyghent	38	1,774	Laddow
10	2,250	Great Coum	39	1,765	Back Tor, Derwent Edge
11	2,239	Crag Hill	40	1,761	Ashop Head
12	2,235	Swarth Fell	41	1,758	Tan Hill
13	2,231	Plover Hill	42	1,750	Edale Cross
14	2,220	The Calf	43	1,696	Mam Tor
15	2,216	East Baugh Fell	44	1,690	Cat and Fiddle
16	2,213	Lovely Seat	45	1,680	The Snake
17	2,191	Fountains Fell	46	1,659	Shuttlingsloe
18	2,189	Dodd Fell Hill	47	1,658	The Roaches
19	2,170	Nine Standards Rigg	48	1,656	Cut Gate
20	2,151	High Cup Nick	49	1,625	Caldron Snout
21	2,109	Yockenthwaite Moor	50	1,569	Butter Tubs
22	2,088	Simon Fell	51	1,563	Lose Hill
23	2,088	Kinder High	52	1,529	Win Hill
24	2,077	Kinder Low	53	1,502	High Neb
25	2,064	Crowden Head	54	1,500	Cowper Stone
26	2,060	Bleaklow Head	55	1,495	Doctor's Gate Culvert
27	2,054	Green Hill	56	1,428	Stanage End
28	2,049	Kinder Edge	57	1,331	Back Tor, Edale
29	2,048	Darnbrook Fell	58	942	Thorpe Cloud

The Peak and Pennine centres

In the following list I have given the principal centres from which the Hills, Dales and Outcrops may be most conveniently reached. But it should be borne in mind that with the almost universal use of the motor car any particular venue can always be attained from more distant places. Even strong walkers without transport should have no difficulty in getting to them, and since the many Youth Hostels are often conveniently situated, hikers who stay in them should experience no insoluble problems of approach. The arrangement of the Centres from south to north follows the same scheme as that adopted throughout the whole of this book.

Dovedale has two hotels near its confluence with the **Manifold**, and other accommodation may be found further away in Fenny Bentley and Ashbourne. There is a Youth Hostel at Ilam Hall and for those who wish to explore the higher reaches of the Dove there is another at Hartington, while a room may also be found in either Longnor or Earl Sterndale.

Black Rocks, Cromford, are at no great distance from the hotels in Matlock and Matlock Bath, while rooms may be found in one or other of the many cottages. There is a Youth Hostel at Matlock.

High Tor overlooks Matlock Bath, to which the last note applies. There is a Youth Hostel at Elton Old Hall.

Robin Hood's Stride and Cratcliff Tor are situated at no great distance from the hotels in Rowsley and Bakewell, while the latter has plenty of other accommodation available.

The Eastern Edges of the Peak District stretch northwards for about fifteen miles from Chatsworth to Derwent, and there are hotels in Baslow and Grindleford Bridge giving access to the southern half and others in Hathersage within easy reach of the northern half. There are also several inns spread along the adjacent valley, as well as the Fox House Inn on the Sheffield Road, while doubtless many of the cottages in the villages could provide accommodation. The nearest Youth Hostel is at Eyam not far from Grindleford.

The Lathkill is about equidistant from the hotels in Rowsley and Bakewell. There are inns at Over Haddon and Youlgreave, and a Youth Hostel at Youlgreave.

The Wye is equally accessible from the hotels in Bakewell and Buxton, and there is also a hotel at Little Longstone above the sharp bend in Monsal Dale. There is a Youth Hostel at Ravenstor in Millers Dale and another in Buxton. Other accommodation can be found in the two towns.

Shining Tor and the Goyt Valley are quite near the famous Cat and Fiddle Inn and those with transport can reach them from the hotels and Youth Hostel in Buxton.

Hen Cloud, Ramshaw Rocks and **The Roaches** may be reached from the hotels in Buxton and Leek. There is no accommodation nearby.

Castleton Caves are all within walking distance of the hotel in the village, where other accommodation may be found in the numerous cottages. There is a Youth Hostel at Castleton Hall.

The Great Ridge separates the Vales of Edale and Hope, and in addition to the accommodation in Castleton there is a hotel and inn at Edale and another at Hope. There is a Youth Hostel at Nether Booth in Edale.

Kinder Scout is usually climbed from Edale where there is a hotel, an inn and a Youth Hostel. The Snake Inn is more distant but useful for the circuit of the mountain. Hayfield is also a starting point for both the ascent and circuit and a bed could doubtless be found in this village.

Doctor's Gate and Bleaklow are usually reached from Glossop, but the Snake Inn could also be used as a base for this expedition.

Laddow is remotely situated but may be attained from either Greenfield or Crowden-in-Longdendale, where accommodation may be found in the Youth Hostel. Climbers with transport could stay as far away as Buxton.

Ilkley lies below the gritstone outcrops which dapple the moor and there are several hotels in the town as well others on the heights above it.

Almscliff is near the villages of Huby and Rigton, but as the Crag is about equidistant from Harrogate, Pool and Otley, ample accommodation may be found.

Brimham Rocks are situated a few miles to the east of Pateley Bridge and due north of Summer Bridge, in both of which villages a bed may be found. Ripon and Ripley are farther away and there are two hotels in the former town; those with transport may prefer to stay there. The Youth Hostel is at Ellingstring not far from Masham.

Wharfedale is resplendent with accommodation throughout its entire length. There are hotels at Bolton Bridge, Burnsall, Grassington, Kettlewell and Buckden, together with several inns and apartments dotted about along the dale bottom. There is a Youth Hostel at Kettlewell, and another at Linton, near Threshfield.

Malham Cove, Tarn and Gordale Scar may be reached on foot from the hotel in Malham, and the John Dower Memorial Hostel is in the village.

Penyghent rises due north-east of Horton-in-Ribblesdale where a bed may be found in the inn or adjacent cottages, while those with transport may prefer to stay in one of the hotels in Settle. There is a Youth Hostel in Stainforth.

Ingleborough may be climbed from the inns at Ingleton or Chapel-le-Dale, but the more interesting route is from the hotel in Clapham by way of Gaping Gill. There is a Youth Hostel at Ingleton.

Whernside may be climbed direct from Chapel-le-Dale Inn, or with transport from Ingleton or Clapham. There is a Youth Hostel at Cowgill in Dentdale. A bed may also be found in either of the above mentioned villages.

Wensleydale has hotels in Aysgarth, Bainbridge and Hawes, and there are inns at Wensley, West Witton, West Burton,

Carperby and Hardrow. A bed may be found in one or other of these villages and there are Youth Hostels in Asygarth near the Falls and at Hawes. **Cautley Spout** is easily reached from Sedbergh where there is ample accommodation.

Butter Tubs can be traversed from the inns at Hardrow or Muker, and the nearest Youth Hostel is at Keld.

Swaledale can be reached from any of the hotels in Richmond, and there are inns at Grinton, Feetham, Gunnerside and Muker. There is a Youth Hostel at Grinton and another at Keld, whence **Tan Hill**, the highest inn in the country, may be attained on foot or by car.

High Force and Caldron Snout. There is a large hotel near the former, and another at Langdon Beck which gives easy access to the latter, first by a paved road and thence on foot. There is a Youth Hostel at Blackton in Baldersdale. Those having transport may prefer to stay further away in one of the hotels in Barnard Castle where apartments are available and there is also a Youth Hostel. Middleton-in-Teesdale is nearer and has a guest house and apartments.

High Cup Nick and Dufton. This picturesque village may be reached from Appleby where there are several hotels, apartments and a guest house.

Cross Fell may be ascended from Kirkland which is the nearest village where a bed might be found. The hotels at Alston and Appleby are some distance away, but the hotel and inn at Melmerby, or the inn at Bradley could give easier access to the starting point of the climb. There is a Youth Hostel at Dufton.

Hadrian's Wall stretches from the Tyne to the Solway, and aside from the varied accommodation to be found in both Newcastle upon Tyne and Carlisle, the whole length of it runs almost parallel with the highway where several towns and villages provide accommodation in hotels, inns and cottages. Those who are particularly interested in Housesteads or the Crag Lough Outcrop could stay at the Twice Brewed inn nearby, whereas others with transport may prefer to sleep at the inns at Gilsland, Greenhead, Haltwhistle, Haydon Bridge,

Bardon Mill or Hexham. There are so many Youth Hostels spread along the entire length of the Wall that reference should be made to the handbook.

Mountain photography

I have already written and lectured extensively on this fascinating branch of photography, and in several of my books I included copious notes on the problems involved in securing good camera studies of many of the Hills and Dales in Britain. But since these books have been out of print for some years, it may be useful to deal more fully with the subject herein, as I have already done in its companion volumes on the Lakeland, Welsh and Scottish Peaks, and in *Climbing with a Camera* which includes the detailed photography of most of the well-known Lakeland Fells. Moreover, I receive innumerable requests for tips from mountaineers who collect my works, and the following summary may provide the desired information and incidentally relieve me of much voluminous correspondence.

1 **The ideal camera for the mountaineer** is undoubtedly the modern miniature owing to its compact form, quick manipulation, great depth of focus, variety of lenses and thirty-six frames on each spool of film. While these instruments are represented in their best and and most expensive type by the Leica, Pentax, Nikon and Canon series, it does not follow that the other less costly makes will not give good photographs. Once I had the opportunity of making a comparative set of colour transparencies with the Leica and a camera that then sold retail for about £12, and had I not been critical I should have been satisfied with the latter; for if you require a camera for your own pleasure and merely wish to show the prints or transparencies to your friends, why pay a great deal for the instrument? In any event, I recommend that you consult your local dealer who will be happy to demonstrate the differences between the various makes and prices.

2 **The lens** is the most important feature, and the best of them naturally facilitate the perfect rendering of the subject. A wide aperture is not essential, because it is seldom necessary to work out of doors at anything greater than F/4.5. It is advisable to use the objective at infinity in mountain photography because overall sharpness is then obtained, and to stop down where required to bring the foreground into focus. It is in this connection that the cheaper camera, which is of course fitted with an inexpensive lens, falls short of its more costly competitors; for the latter are corrected for every known fault and the resulting photographs are then not only acceptable for enlarged reproduction but also yield exhibition prints of superlative quality. Three lenses are desirable in this branch of photography: 1. a 28mm or 35mm wide angle; 2. a standard 50mm which is usually supplied with most cameras; and 3. a 90mm long focus. These cover every likely requirement: the wide angle is most useful when *on* a mountain or lofty ridge; the 50mm encompasses the average scene, such as hill and dale; and the long focus is an advantage when the subject is very distant.

An analysis of their use in this extensive region is as follows:

Wide angle	40 per cent
Standard	55 per cent
Long focus	5 per cent

3 **A lens hood** is an indispensable accessory, because it cuts out adventitious light and increases the brilliance and clarity of the picture. Many climbers have the illusion that this gadget is only required when the sun is shining and that it is used to keep the direct rays out of the lens when facing the light source. While its use is then imperative, they overlook the fact that light is reflected from many points of the hemisphere around the optical axis, and it is the interception of this incidental light that is important.

4 **A filter** is desirable, especially for the good rendering of skyscapes. A pale orange yields the most dramatic results, providing there are not vast areas of trees in the landscape in which all detail would be lost. It is safer to use a yellow filter, which does not suffer from this defect, and with autumn colours a green filter is very effective. The *exposure factors* do not differ materially, and in view of the wide latitude of modern monochrome film the resulting slight differences in density can be corrected when printing. *For colour work* a skylight filter, formerly known as a Wratten 1A, was useful for reducing the intensity of the blues and for eliminating haze, but from recent experiments with several makes of colour film I have found its use to be no longer necessary owing to improvements in manufacture.

5 **Panchromatic film** is to be preferred for landscapes, and the speed of modern types has been increased substantially, so much so that an ASA rating of up to 125 will yield grainless negatives providing they are processed with the developer that is recommended by the makers.

6 **Exposure and development** are co-related. From May to September with bright sunlight and well distributed clouds, films of the above speed require an average exposure of 1/250th of a second at an aperture of F/8 or 11 with a 2 × yellow filter, processed with a fine-grain developer for eight minutes at a temperature of 68°F. Such negatives should be brilliantly clear and not too contrasty, and they will print on normal paper.

7 **The best time of year** for photography in the Backbone of England are the months of April and May. A limpid atmosphere and fine cumulus are then a common occurence and less time is wasted in waiting for favourable lighting. Moreover, during April many of the higher hills may be dressed in snowy raiment which adds sparkle and glamour and transforms them into peaks of Alpine splendour. Colour

Plate 2 Clouds over Ingleborough

work at these times is also satisfactory because the landscape still reveals the reds of the dead bracken, which, however, disappear in June with the rapid growth of the new fresh green fronds. Nevertheless, the most dramatic colour transparencies are obtained during the last week of October because the newly dead bracken is then a fiery red, the grass has turned to golden yellow, and the longer shadows increase the contrast between hill and dale.

8 **Lack of sharpness** is a problem that causes disappointment to some climbers, and they are often apt to blame the lens when the defect is in fact due to camera shake. It is one thing to hold the instrument steady at ground level with a good stance and no strong wind to disturb the balance, while it is quite another problem in the boisterous breezes on the lofty hills and moors. When these conditions prevail, it is risky to use a lower speed than that indicated above, and maximum stability may be achieved by leaning against a slab of rock or in a terrific gale of wind by even lying down and jamming the elbows into the spaces between the crags. In calm weather a light tripod may be used, but in all other conditions it is too risky to erect one and have it blown over a precipice!

9 **Lighting** is the key to fine mountain photography, and the sun at an angle of 45 degrees, over the left or right shoulder, will yield the required contrasts. These conditions usually obtain in the early morning or the late evening. If possible avoid exposures at midday with the sun overhead when the lighting is flat and uninteresting. Before starting on any climb, study the topography of your mountain so that full advantage can be taken of the lighting. Moreover, never be persuaded to discard your camera when setting out in bad weather, because the atmosphere in the hills is subject to the most sudden and unexpected changes, and sometimes wet mornings develop into fine afternoons, with magnificent clouds and limpid lighting. If your camera is then back in your lodgings, you may live to regret the omission.

10 **The sky** is often the saving feature in mountain photographs since cloudless conditions or a sunless landscape seldom yield a pleasing picture. But to capture a fine cloud formation as well as the subject in the same frame often means the tilting of the camera upwards and sacrificing the foreground. The example of Ingleborough (plate 2) is perhaps exceptional because it was taken some distance to the south and should be compared with plate 195, taken from the north, where the inclusion of the whole mountain was of greater importance than the sky.

11 **Haze** is one of the bugbears in this branch of photography, and these conditions are especially prevalent in the Peak and Pennines during July and August. If an opalescent effect is desired, this is the time of year to secure it, but while such camera studies may be favoured by the purist, they seldom appeal to the climber who prefers to see the detail he knows exists in his subjects.

12 **Colour photography** has been simplified in recent years by the introduction of cameras in which both exposure and aperture can be automatically adjusted to light conditions, and in consequence failures are rare. Owing to the narrow latitude of colour film correct exposure is essential if the resulting transparency is to approximate in hue to that of the landscape as seen by the eye. The only certain way to achieve success in all weather conditions is to *use a meter before making each exposure* and to be sure it is pointed at the same angle as the camera. This is most important, because if more sky is included in the meter than in the lens a shorter exposure will be indicated and this will result in an under-exposed transparency in which the colour will be unduly intensified, whereas if the two operations are reversed it will be weakened. Excellent results are obtainable with most makes of colour film, whose speed has been substantially increased in recent years. ASA10 used to be the standard, whereas today ASA25, 32, 64 and 100 are in common use. On the basis of ASA25, an

exposure of about 1/125th of a second at an aperture of F/8 in sunlight between 10 a.m. and 4 p.m. in the summer yields superlative transparencies which are viewed to greatest advantage by projection. The correct exposure for other ASA speeds may be readily calculated from a good exposure meter.

The dramatic possibilities of photographing sunsets in colour are worthy of study, and such scenes are enhanced by placing a still or slightly rippling sheet of water in the foreground which captures the colour reflected by water as well as that already appearing in the sky. But meter readings of these subjects are often unreliable and I have found that for films of ASA25 an exposure of 1/60th of a second at an aperture of F/4.5 gives perfect results.

13 **Design or composition** is the most outstanding feature of a good camera study; that is, one that not only immediately appeals to the eye, but rather one that can be lived with afterwards. Everything I have so far written herein on this subject comes within the scope of *technique*, and anyone who is prepared to give it adequate study and practice should be able to produce a good negative, and from it a satisfying print.

But to create a picture that far transcends even the best snapshot requires more than this and might well be described as a flair, or if you like a seeing eye that immediately appreciates the artistic merits of a particular mountain scene. And strangely enough those who possess this rare gift usually produce a certain type of picture which is indelibly stamped with their personality; so much so that it is often possible to name the photographer as soon as his work is displayed. And, moreover, while this especial artistic trait may be developed after long application of the basic principles of composition, the fact remains that it is not the camera that really matters, for it is merely a tool, but the person behind the viewfinder, who, when satisfied with the design of his subject, ultimately and quite happily releases the shutter.

To the painter, composition is relatively easy, because he

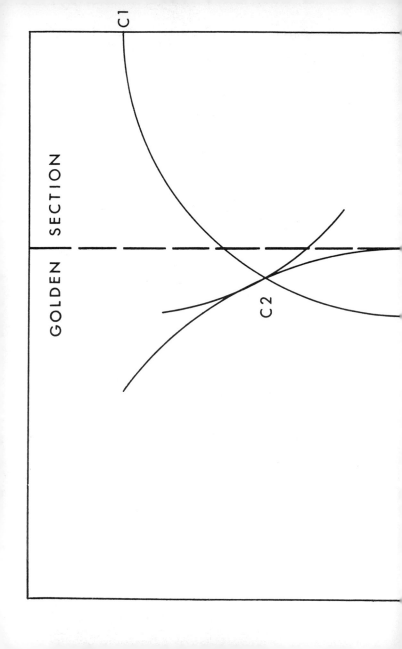

Plate 3 Back Tor

can make it conform to the basic principles of art by moving a tree to one side of his picture, or by completely removing a house from the foreground, or by inducing a stream to flow in another direction, or by accentuating the real subject, if it happens to be a mountain, by moving it or by increasing or decreasing its angles to suit his tastes. A photographer on the other hand has to move himself and his camera here and there in order to get these objects in the right position in his viewfinder. When he moves to one side to improve the position of one of them, another is thrown out of place, or perhaps the lighting is altered. In many cases, therefore, a compromise is the only solution, because if he spends too much time in solving his problem the mood may change, when his opportunity would be lost. It is just this element in mountain photography that brings it into line with sport, and, like golf, it can be both interesting and exasperating. Of course, the critic can sit in a comfortable chair by a warm fire at home and pull a photograph to pieces. He does not, perhaps, realise that the person taking the picture may have been wandering about knee-deep in a slimy bog, or that a bitterly cold wind was sweeping across a lofty moor and making his teeth chatter, or that the light was failing, or that he had crawled out on a rocky spur with a hundred-foot drop on either side to get his subject properly composed.

Assuming, therefore, both lighting and cloudscape are favourable, what are the essential features of good composition? In the first place, you must select a pleasing object that is accentuated by tonal contrast as the centre of interest; in the second you must place this object in the most attractive position in the frame or picture space; and in the third you must choose a strong and appropriate foreground. or, in other words, when the weather is favourable the success or failure of your photograph will depend entirely upon the *viewpoint*.

Finally, whenever you take a photograph of any of the Pennine Peaks, remember that it will be improved not only by placing a stream, a bridge, a figure or a group of climbers in the foreground, but also on occasion by introducing a tree or cottage or some object whose size if known will impart both interest and scale to your picture

Before leaving this interesting question of design or composition, it might be helpful to mention two systems that are used for arriving at the strongest placing of the subject in the frame. The favoured picture space measures 2×3, 4×6, 20×30 and so on, or as in the miniature camera 24×36, and when it is divided into thirds the horizontal lines cut the verticals at four points. To obtain a balance that satisfies the eye, the subject, such as a mountain peak, should be placed with its summit on one of the upper points, and an object such as a cairn, a cottage, a tree or a figure on the lower opposite point. This raises a problem when the subject is not well defined, as when a peak does not stand alone but is confused by other adjacent mountains which cannot be excluded from the picture space. In such instances the design must be left to the photographer who will do his best to strike a balance that pleases the eye. And while it is a simple matter for anyone to guess at the thirds when looking through the viewfinder, the other system favoured by such great artists as El Greco, Leonardo, Raphael and Tintoretto, is much more difficult to position precisely, although as shown by the accompanying drawing and study of Back Tor, it can be acquired approximately by practice and is acknowledged as the ideal in design. In fact, placing the subject on the *golden section* gives a perfect visual satisfaction to the observer. There is a feeling of balance and order, even excitement in dramatic conditions—the interest is demanded.

The method of finding the approximate *golden section* is as follows: draw a frame measuring 4×6 inches and bisect the base line A B at C. With B as the centre and radius B C, draw an arc that intersects the vertical edge at C1. With C1 as the centre and the same radius B C intersect C-C1 at C2. From A with A-C2 as the radius, find the Golden Section where it reaches the base line at G S. This vertical line rising from G S was called the 'divine proportion' by no less an artist than

Leonardo, who considered the frame should be so divided in order to communicate most successfully through the eye an arrangement of shapes, dimensions and directions, mass and counter mass, that would solicit, hold and move the attention and interest.

The subject in the example is shown on the right, but is of course equally applicable on the left, and moreover, the same system can be applied to vertical frames, or to the more common whole plate, $8\frac{1}{2} \times 6\frac{1}{2}$ inches, or to exhibition prints measuring 15×12 inches or 20×16 inches.

Note: In order to adapt the 24×36 negatives to the sizes required in this volume, it has sometimes been necessary to reduce, or even omit, the foreground appearing in the original photographs.

Some useful photographic hints

There are several photographic problems that are peculiar to this region and they are seldom encountered elsewhere in our British Hills. The first of them worthy of note concerns the prolific growth of trees during the last twenty years, a development which has completely changed some of the fine scenery and nowadays interferes with its satisfactory photography. An outstanding example is that of Dovedale, whose narrow defile from the Stepping Stones to Ilam Rock— is so overcrowded with trees and a tangle of dense undergrowth that while the river can be dimly perceived in the gloom most of the splendid tors and pinnacles of limestone that rise on either side of the dale cannot be seen in their entirety or photographed in their full beauty. In fact, the one-time splendour of the prospect from Sharplow Point is so cluttered up that only the tops of the Tissington Spires are now visible.

Another example is that of Middleton Dale, where the long line of limestone precipices on the north side of the dale adjacent to Stoney Middleton is largely hidden by a prolific display of trees and a vast tangle of undergrowth. While it is true that these may give welcome cover to the climbers who camp at the base of the cliffs, the fact remains that the grandeur of this spectacular wall of vertical limestone is no longer visible and can only be seen in part even from the quarries opposite. A further example is that of Chee Dale, but here the trees do not encroach too much and the limestone eminences that hem in the narrowest section of the dale can be observed above them.

The Edges and Outcrops are not completely immune, although it must be admitted that most of them are fortunately poised above the tree line and are thus easily photographed. Robin Hood's Stride and the Black Rocks of Cromford are hopelessly engulfed and sections of the magnificent Roaches also suffer from this disadvantage, but happily the dominating feature of the Sloth is free from any serious encroachment at present. The best way to photograph the splendour of the Edges is to walk along their crests in one direction and return along their base in the other. Moreover, it should be noted that since most of them face the west or south-west, a sunny afternoon is the best time for such an enjoyable promenade. Rock climbing photographs are not always easily secured, although the above hint will often facilitate the taking of effective shots. In some cases it is advisable, and in others indeed necessary, to scale the adjacent cliff face in order to get the best pictures of the climbers at work.

Cave Photography is a specialised art and involves the use of flash. In larger caverns, such as the immense Chamber below Gaping Gill, as much as a pound of magnesium may be necessary to impart sufficient illumination for a satisfactory exposure. In the smaller caves ordinary flash bulbs give good results, but it is advisable to place the camera on a tripod, focus on the subject, stop the lens down to $F/11$ or 16 and then open the shutter. According to the size and distance of the subject one or more flash bulbs may then be used from a position on one side or the other to impart contrast and reveal all the detail in the stalagmite, stalactite or other picturesque formation. If the cave is wet, with water dripping from the limestone roof, great care is essential in order to avoid it falling on the camera, otherwise the viewfinder may cloud up with condensation of moisture and the mechanism of the shutter may be modified to such an extent that its speeds are altered with dire consequences to both colour and monochrome film.

Notes on the Routes

I have arranged the Peak and Pennines from south to north for the sake of convenience and easy reference. They commence with Dovedale, continue along the eastern Outcrops and Edges and return to the Lathkill and Wye followed by the outcrops to the south of Buxton. Thence from Castleton and the Great Ridge they include both Kinder and Bleaklow, and end with Laddow as the last feature of interest in the Peak District National Park. The Pennines begin with the outcrops within range of Ilkley and then pass on to Wharfedale, thereafter visiting Malham on the way to Penyghent, Ingleborough and Whernside. From Wensleydale, Butter Tubs goes over the hills to Swaledale and Tan Hill, whence the Tees leads to High Cup Nick and Dufton. Cross Fell is the last ascent and the work terminates with Hadrian's Wall.

Ascents – When there is more than one route to the dominating peak in a group of hills, I have described the most popular one first, followed by the alternatives, in which case the reversal of one of them could be used for the *descent*.

The panorama from the reigning peak in each group is always noted at the termination of its first ascent. But many of the routes involve the traverse of subsidiary tops and the conspicuous features revealed from them are mentioned in passing, despite the fact that there may be a similarity in the views when they are near together.

Distances and times

These questions always involve a certain amount of speculation in mountaineering and I have purposely omitted any detailed reference to them in his work. *The distances* may be calculated from the maps, which are approximately one inch to the mile, but it should be remembered that a map mile may in fact be considerably more than that owing to the undulating nature of the ground. *The times* depend not only upon the pace and rhythm of each climber, but also upon the topography of the mountain as well as weather conditions. The best way to calculate them is to use the formula of Naismith, which allows one hour for each three map miles, plus half an hour for every 1,000 feet of ascent. This is fairly accurate for ordinary hill walking under favourable conditions, and while it includes reasonable halts for food and for viewing the grandeur of the mountain scene, it does not allow for bad weather, snow, rock climbing or photography, since the latter often involves much delay in finding the most effective foreground for any particular picture and for awaiting favourable lighting.

Route finding in mist

In these not uncommon conditions it is imperative to know with certainty your exact location on the map when mist comes down to engulf you in gloom and to immediately note the direction to be taken. If you are on a well-cairned track no difficulties should be encountered, but when this is not the case you must estimate the distance to the next known point and set a course accurately by using your companion as a sighting mark. Keep him in view ahead while frequently referring to the compass and use your aneroid to check the rise and fall in the ground. If you are familiar with the gradient this will help to control your direction, but take nothing for granted; always trust the compass excepting when among magnetic rocks, basaltic and gabbro formations such as exist in the Coolins of Skye, and pay no attention whatsoever to gratuitous advice as to the direction from compassless companions. Avoid contouring a slope; if you do this, you will no longer be master of your direction. It is always advisable to go straight down and never diverge from a supposed obstacle without actual trial, because mist exaggerates both size and distance.

Should you be in the unhappy position of having no compass but are *familiar with the terrain*, work your way down slowly over grass but never enter a ravine or gully or endeavour to descend a series of steep crags, whereas if you are on a ridge keep to its declining crest and if it forks make sure you take the known branch. If, on the other hand, you are alone on an uncairned hill and also unfamiliar with the ground, stay put until the mist clears sufficiently for you to find your way. In these conditions you are in a very dangerous situation because mist sometimes persists for days in mountainous country. It is much better to practise map and compass reading in clear weather so that in mist you will have a reasonable chance of finding your way to safety.

Accident procedure

Distress signal. *Six* long flashes or *six* long blasts of a whistle in quick succession followed by a pause of one minute. This is repeated again and again until assistance is forthcoming.

The reply to this signal is in a similar vein; that is *three* flashes or blasts of a whistle followed by a pause of one minute, repeated again and again.

Brocken spectres

These remarkable phenomena are usually confined to hill country, and in consequence may, with luck, be observed by any climber on the Pennine Peaks, especially if he happens to be on a lofty edge enclosing a coombe filled with mist. They appear as gigantic shadows on the surface of the mist and were first observed on the Brocken in Germany, hence the name, but are said to be an optical illusion because the shadow is quite close and of actual size. It is usually only possible for each climber to see his own spectre.

Glories

These appear as a coloured ring round the shadow cast by the climber on the mist in similar circumstances. Each member of a climbing party can see only his own glory. Readers who have flown in an aeroplane will have often seen the shadow of the plane ringed by a variegated circle on the clouds beneath them.

The Pennine Way

After many years of trials, tribulations and difficult problems of access, the sinuous route of this 250-mile-long high-level walk, though given legal effect in 1951, was finally completed in 1965. There is little doubt that the successful issue of these long deliberations was due to the late Mr Tom Stephenson. Starting in Edale in the Peak District, the Pennine Way winds its way through the northern counties of England, finally to reach the Scottish border at Kirk Yetholm. It not only takes in the most interesting, wild and scenic features of the Backbone of England, but each of its sections have also been arranged to terminate at spots where accommodation is readily available in villages and Youth Hostels, save in a few places where they are rather distant. Any experienced walker who embarks upon this long hill traverse in fine weather should be able to complete it in a fortnight, or at most in seventeen days. And although numerous signposts, cairns and stakes have been placed in key positions along the Way, it will be obvious that a study of the relevant maps is essential before starting out. The following summary is taken from the detailed route published by the Ramblers' Association, and those who are interested should acquire a copy which has the advantage of indicating the Sheet Numbers of the Ordnance Survey one-inch maps, seventh edition, applicable to each section.

The Pennine Way leaves Edale by Grindsbrook and on attaining the Kinder plateau it passes to the west of Crowden Head, whence the Kinder River leads to the Downfall. It then descends to Mill Hill, crosses Featherbed Top for the highest point of the Snake Road, whence it goes over Doctor's Gate to Devil's Dike and thereafter round the head of Crooked Clough to Bleaklow Head.

Descending the north side of this moorland wilderness, the route passes Torside Castle and Clough Edge to the foot of the reservoir at A628. On the other side of the road it follows a path up the Crowden Valley to Laddow and then up the rising ground to Black Hill, descending thence to A635, and after passing between the Wessenden reservoirs it turns west to Standedge on A62 where it leaves the Peak District National Park.

Crossing Castleshaw Moor, the Way leads to A640 and thence by the Lancashire-West Riding boundary to White Hill, and beyond A672 Blackstone Edge to White House Inn on A58. A path now continues to the farthest reservoir and by Warland Drain to Stoodley Pike, and after passing Edge End Moor goes down to A646. Continuing thence to the Halifax reservoir, the track goes to Withens, the supposed original of *Wuthering Heights*, to Ponden reservoir and later over Keighley Moor to Pinhaw Beacon, whence by Gargrave and down to Thornton and Eshton Moor and then along the banks of the Aire to Malham.

Leaving behind Malham Cove, a footpath goes over Prior Rakes, passes Malham Tarn House, crosses the moor to Tennant Gill, rises along the flanks of Fountains Fell, passes its Tarn on the L and then descends to Silverdale at Dale Head, whence the summit of Penyghent is attained. The wall on the ridge is followed in the direction of Plover Hill and on reaching the dip the Way turns L and descends the old quarry track and follows the stream to Hunt Pot and thence to Horton-in-Ribblesdale.

Proceeding north by a grassy track to Sell Gill Holes and thence towards Birkwith Moor where it twists L and later R for Cam Beck, it keeps to the west side of Dodd Fell to Gayle and Hawes. Crossing Wensleydale to Hardrow, it takes the old mine track to Black Hill Moss and thence over Greater Shunner Fell to Thwaite in Upper Swaledale, thereafter ascending round the east side of Kisdon and later dropping down to Kisdon Force for Keld.

The Way now follows the old road through Stonesdale to Tan Hill Inn and then bears R for Sleightholme, and later by Trough Heads and God's Bridge to Pasture End on A66. On the other side of this busy highway, it goes north to Ravock Castle and crosses Deepdale to the head of Baldersdale reservoir. Thence from High Birk Hat it passes Lunedale reservoir, Nettlepot, Wythes Hill and Old Quarry to Middleton-in-Teesdale. Here it crosses the Tees to the Yorkshire side and follows the stream to Holwick Head House, passes High Force and joins the path to Cronkley. It now crosses the bridge to Durham Bank and keeps to Langdon Beck as far as New House, and thence by Widdybank Farm to Caldron Snout. Thereafter the track takes a westerly course to the lonely farm of Birkdale, passes Moss Shop and rises up the valley of Maize Beck through some of the most desolate stretches of the Pennines before descending from High Cup Nick to Dufton.

From this picturesque village the Way rises to Green Fell and Knock Fell, whence it passes over Great and Little Dun Fells to attain Cross Fell. From the north-west corner of the Screes it takes in Crossfell Well, goes down to the mine track and then follows a long north eastern descent to Garrygill. Thereafter it keeps to the river as far as Sillyhall and by footpath to Alston Bridge, and thence to Castle Nook by crossing and re-crossing B6292.

The route continues by Maiden Way to Slaggyford and rejoins it later along the lower flanks of Glendue Fell, eventually to reach A69(T) after crossing Hartleyburn Common. Thereafter it goes on to Thirlwall Castle and so reaches Hadrian's Wall. It now keeps to the Roman Wall over Winshields Crags and Crag Lough to within half a mile beyond Housesteads where it turns north to follow a sinuous course through Wark Forest to Bellingham.

The Way now goes due north from the Youth Hostel via Blakelow to B6320, and after crossing the highway takes a north-westerly direction to Lord's Shaw, beyond which it crosses a road for Padon Hill and then through a forestry plantation to Blakehopeburnhaugh and Byrness. Thence it goes on to the Roman Camp at Chew Green and north by Dere Street to reach the border near Raeshaw Fell which it follows to Cheviot and subsequently to Kirk Yetholm. At the time of writing the record for this walk was held by Joss

Naylor who did it in 3 days, 4 hours and 35 minutes.

Many of the outstanding landmarks on the Pennine Way are described and illustrated in the following pages and wherever possible a reference is made to its course in those of the 59 Routes that are applicable. You may consult as well *A guide to the Pennine Way* by Christopher John Wright, also published by Constable.

Dovedale

It is now more than forty years since I first set foot in this lovely dale. It was a beautiful autumn day, with a blue sky lightly flecked with clouds, and the trees were assuming their golden tapestry while the stream cascaded quietly over the moss-covered weirs to make sweet music. As I strolled along the path beside this anglers' paradise, the limestone pinnacles on either side of the dale gleamed brightly in the sunshine and the last of them—Ilam Rock— was then draped with clinging ivy and scarcely regarded seriously by rock climbers after the fright of Herford. I continued through the wider section which follows, past Dove Holes where the dale proper ends, crossed the old packhorse bridge in Milldale and then entered the less picturesque stretches of Wolfscote Dale to be charmed finally by Beresford Dale, with its conspicuous pinnacle rising from the silent Pike Pool. In the intervening period I have visited Dovedale twice, in spring and in the winter, and on each occasion it was a rare experience to meet many walkers enjoying this galaxy of river, tree and rock.

I returned to this dale one early September day in the 1960s to revive and check these pleasant memories so that I could give an up-to-date account in these pages. There were several surprises in store; for an immense car park below the Izaak Walton Hotel was crowded, hundreds of people were wandering through the dale together with parties of curious and happy children with their schoolteachers, and the rapid growth of the forest of trees had marred the views of the limestone tors and pinnacles that grace this pageant of Nature. However, Ilam Rock, now bereft of its ivy, had drawn parties of climbers who were making a mechanised ascent of this leaning pinnacle, but the nearby canopy of trees made it difficult to photograph them in action. This appeared to be the terminal point of the pedestrians, for the dale was empty beyond it. It would seem, therefore, that Dovedale will always be one of the greatest attractions in the Peak District,

ton Hill
Paddock Ho.
Narrowdale
The Whim
O N A
Gratton Hill
Manor Ho.
Gateham Grange
Gateham
NT
312m
Steep Low
Under Wetton
Alstonfield
Mill
Wetton Hill
Hope
NT
Wetton
Milldale
OR'S CAVE
Wetton Low
Hopedale
1a
The Grove
Stanshope
Beeston Tor
Oldpark Hill
NT
Damgate NT
Hamps Rock
Dove Holes
Throwley Hall
R. Castern
Manifold
Hall
Twelve Apostles
Throwley Cottage
Rushley
Bunster Hill
Slade Ho.
Musden Grange
Ilam
NT Hall
Izaak Walton Hotel
YH
Nature Trail
1

Map 1
Dovedale and Manifold

and of course the river, which rises over fifty miles away on Axe Edge, near Buxton, will continue to be the delight of the angler.

Another development in Dovedale has been the increase in rock climbing during the past decade which was formerly confined to Ilam Rock and to the adjacent Pickering Tor. The former is like a gigantic limestone tooth and routes occur on three of its four faces. There are three climbs, including the Original, on the north and west faces, and four on the south face. Of these the White Edge is the most spectacular, taking the extreme right side of the face above the river. All the crags between Milldale and Thorpe Cloud have now been climbed.

In view of the previously mentioned growth of the trees in the dale, whilst this edition was in preparation I asked my son to visit the area and report on the present situation. He was only able to go there in November when all the trees were bare, but he viewed the subjects of all the plates in this section and came to the conclusion that only two were seriously affected by the present height of the trees; plate 5 — *The Entrance to Dovedale*, and plate 11 — *Ilam Rock*. Due to the sun being low at that time of the year, it was impossible for him to rephotograph these satisfactorily, but he feels that by moving the viewpoints good pictures may still be obtained. Extensive clearance of trees and undergrowth has now revealed Tissington Spires in all their glory, in a carefully planned scheme.

Route 1. Leave the Buxton-Ashbourne highway by the side road opposite the entrance to Tissington, and drive carefully downhill past Peveril of the Peak, beyond which the conical grassy eminence of Thorpe Cloud comes into view. Cross the little bridge and turn R beside the river, past the Izaak Walton Hotel on the L, and enter the commodious car park.

Begin your walk by going towards the V-shaped gap between the dale's guarding sentinels—Bunster on the L and Thorpe Cloud on the R—and if you wish to avoid the dizzy crossing of the Stepping Stones from Staffordshire into

Derbyshire, go over the bridge on the R and follow the path beside the stream. The dale soon bends sharply to the north-west immediately to reveal its sylvan character, with a variety of dense trees often running up to the skyline. As you walk along the greensward beside the quiet Dove, note on the L the Castle Rocks and then the Twelve Apostles, whence the path rises gently to Sharplow Point, with the Lovers' Leap on the L. This is the highest point of the path and it opens up a fine vista of the dale ahead, in which Tissington Spires may be clearly seen on the R. Rest awhile to enjoy the view and then continue downhill to the L bank of the Dove, pass the base of the Spires on the R leading to Reynard's Cave. Thereafter the dale narrows considerably to what is called the Straits where it is dominated on the R by the Lion's Head Rock; the space is so confined that there is barely room for river and path which leads to Pickering Tor on the R and eventually to Ilam Rock on the L. Here there is a footbridge and paths on either side of the stream lead shortly to more open ground, on the R of which appear Dove Holes, the end proper of Dovedale. Some readers may wish to continue this enchanting walk to Hartington, while others may prefer to return by way of Wetton and Thor's Cave, a remarkable cavern on the hillside whose lofty arched roof is supported by massive limestone columns.

Plate 4 **Route 1**—Thorpe Cloud

Plate 5 **Route 1** — The entrance to Dovedale

Plate 6 **Route 1** — Crossing the Stepping Stones

Plate 7 **Route 1**—The Dove below Castle Rocks

Plate 8 **Route 1**—Natural Arch below Reynard's Cave

Plate 9 **Route 1**— The Lion Rock

Plate 10 **Route 1**—Pickering Tor

Plate 11 **Route 1**—Ilam Rock

Plate 12 **Route 1**—Dove Holes, the end of Dovedale proper

The Manifold Valley

After the enchanting walk in Dovedale, visitors who are not pressed for time should drive to Ilam which is delightfully situated in the Manifold Valley. It has a fine Cross surrounded by trim and charming Gothic cottages and also one of the best youth Hostels in Britain; Ilam Hall, an Elizabethan Mansion of the last century. Its beautiful gardens are of special interest because the subterranean stretches of the Manifold River reappear in them and the bubbling waters issuing from the limestone may be seen by descending to the narrow valley behind the Hall.

Route 1a. Thor's Cave is the most interesting feature of this valley and it is easily reached by continuing the drive to Wetton and thereafter by walking along the track beyond the village which crosses the hillside to its large opening in the face of the cliff where the steep approach has been eased by a long line of steps. The best distant view of the cave is obtained from the lofty section of the road to Butterton, as shown in plate 14. This Cave possesses several remarkable features; the arch is symmetrical, 23 feet wide and 30 feet high, with its floor 250 feet above the now dry river bed. The cave is effectively illuminated to a considerable depth by a second narrow and lofty opening on the R, opposite which stands a massive column supporting the arches penetrating still further into the grim recesses of the hillside. Moreover, the proportions are magnificent and the entrance commands an extensive prospect of the hills to the north. It is one of the sights of the district and should be visited by all rock climbers who will doubtless agree that the roof climb, known as Kyrie Eleison, used to be one of the hardest aid climbs in the Peak District National Park.

Plate 13 **Route 1a**—Ilam Cross and cottages

Plate 14 **Route 1a**— Thor's Cave

Plate 15 **Route 1a**—The symmetrical arch of Thor's Cave

Plate 16 **Route 1a**—Massive column supporting the arches in Thor's Cave

The Black Rocks of Cromford

This striking outcrop of gritstone is a conspicuous landmark
almost on the edge of Cromford Moor and is situated a little
over a mile to the south of the village. Walkers may reach it
by following the Wirksworth Road and then crossing the
moor on the L near a small house, while those with transport
will drive further up the hill towards a low bridge and turn L
along a rough road which ends in a large car park almost
opposite the famous Railway Slab. The popularity of this
bold escarpment is indicated by a wide scree track which rises
to its north-west corner. The High Peak Mineral Line skirts
the hillside well below the rocks and it is an easy ascent to the
wide commanding platform which unfolds a comprehensive
panorama of the Matlock district. On attaining this lofty
coign of vantage it will be noted that the colour of the rocks is
scarcely black and their designation thus misleading; for since
they face the north the sunlight is always behind them, and as
they are silhouetted against the sky they appear to be black
and forbidding. Moreover, this contrast in colour is
emphasised by the pale hue of the surrounding limestone
landscape.

The Black Rocks are a picturesque group of crags and in
their small compass epitomise all varieties of gritstone climbs.
They are uniformly steep and of sound and rough
construction, but while they are clean on a dry day they
acquire a film of sandy mud in wet weather and the quantities
of sand in the gullies suggests a rapid rate of erosion. This has
left five huge bastions, each exhibiting a strange and varied
beauty and occupying a dominating position with a northern
aspect, whereas the western extremity is an unbroken wall
split by grooves and cracks. Forty years ago the trees below
them were scanty and all their features were visible, whereas
today the rapid growth of trees has obscured some of them,
leaving only those portrayed in the accompanying
photograph. From R to L they are: Birch Tree Wall, Finale
Wall, Sand Buttress, Stonnis Arete and the Promontory;

Map 2
Rock Outcrops

those now hidden are Centre Buttress, Queen's Parlour Slab, New Year Buttress and East Buttress. The maximum length of the vertical routes is not more than ninety feet, although a Girdle Traverse has been worked out and involves some 270 feet of climbing. All the starting points of the ascents may be reached from a path which runs along the base of the crags.

Route 2. Drive south along the main road from Matlock Bath, passing on the L the prominent limestone outcrop of High Tor whose 79 climbs are among the greatest in the Peak District and are much frequented. On emerging from the gorge turn R for Cromford and then L for Wirksworth Road. Leave the vehicle in the car park near the Railway Slab, and walk up the broad scree track to the summit platform for the spacious view round the northern arc, and observe the conspicuous Stonnis Pinnacle below its crest. Then descend and walk along the base of the crags, noting the well-known routes from west to east; Lone Tree Groove and Birch Tree Wall on the short but steep west face; now turn R for the long broken northern face for Fat Man's Chimney, Sand Gully, Sand Buttress, Stonnis Crack, Stonnis Arete, Garden Wall Traverse, Centre Buttress, Queen's Parlour, New Year Buttress and East Buttress. Near Birch Tree Wall are some of the hardest modern gritstone climbs, including Gaa, which takes an impossible-looking groove.

Plate 17 Gymnastics on the Railway Slab

Plate 18 **Route 2** — Matlock–Riber Castle and High Tor

Plate 19 **Route 2**—The Black Rocks of Cromford

Plate 20 **Route 2**. The Western Face : Gaa climbs the front of the left-hand boulder

Plate 21 **Route 2** — The summit platform

Cratcliff Tor

This fine gritstone outcrop is a conspicuous object rising to the west of the Winster Road and is about one mile from Birchover. A cart track to its south leads to a rustic farmstead situated almost at the foot of the Tor. This is characterised by a uniformly steep face of sound and clean rock over 100 feet high. At its south-west corner, two yews mark the position of the famous Hermit's Cave which is railed in and contains a crucifix. The Hermitage Crack rises to the R of it and leads up to the Hermitage Chimney. then comes the Giant's Staircase which yields eighty feet of climbing and is marked by an oak and a Spanish chestnut. The Amphitheatre lies to the R and its floor is raised above the foot of the Tor. Near the middle there is an easy way to the top of the crag, but this platform can also be attained by a path through the trees on the L. The most famous climbs take the buttresses on either side of Owl Gully, including Suicide Wall, Requiem, Five Finger Exercise and Fernhill. Owl Gully is the conspicuous V-shaped rift splitting the prominent buttress from base to summit on the R of the Amphitheatre.

Route 3. Any observant traveller proceeding north from Winster in the direction of Rowsley or Bakewell will note, on coming downhill, the dominating gritstone outcrop of Cratcliff Tor on the far horizon. This stands well above the trees, but its near neighbour, Robin Hood's Stride, is so overgrown as to be identified only with difficulty. When the road levels out park your car in the side road or if there is no room leave it on the grass verge of the main road nearby. now go through the gate or stile and walk straight ahead to the Tor.

Plate 22 **Route 3**—Cratcliff Tor

Robin Hood's Stride

Sometimes called Mock Beggars Hall, this remarkable gritstone outcrop stands in more open ground to the west of Cratcliff Tor, but numerous trees growing among its maze of boulders rather mar its fine appearance. It is characterised by two fluted pinnacles which are some thirty feet apart, so Robin Hood must have been a veritable giant to have stepped across the gap between them. To climbers they are known respectively as the Inaccessible, which is the larger one of the west, and as the Weasel, which stands nearer Cratcliff Tor. Paths from every side give access to the platform between the pinnacles.

Route 4. Follow Route 3 nearly to the farmstead and turn L up a cart track which leads direct to the Stride. Scramble up to the platform and observe the view to the west which is extensive and clearly reveals the rolling uplands of the Peak. If you are bound for the enchanting Lathkill, walk along the path in a north-westerly direction behind the Stride which gives access to the lane running downhill to Alport. On the R of the path, and some short distance from the lane, stands one of the most remarkable Stone Circles in the Stanton Moor district. If you make this diversion, you will note that there are only four stones on their beam-ends in this one, although it was formerly known as Nine Stones.

Plate 23 **Route 4**— Robin Hood's Stride

Plate 24 **Route 4**—Inaccessible Pinnacle

Plate 25 **Route 4**—Weasel Pinnacle

Plate 26 **Route 4**—Looking across the Stride

The Edges

The eastern Edges of the Peak are a unique feature of our
British Hills, and extend northwards for some fifteen miles
along the lofty rim of the Derwent Valley from Chatsworth to
Ladybower Reservoir. To the east they are bounded by
extensive stretches of bleak moorland, to which they form the
precipitous lip, and to the west the ground sinks down
gradually to the streams that thread the valley floor. These
slopes are usually strewn with boulders and scree and only
occasionally shagged with trees, but they are decked with
heather and bracken which enhances the views of them from
above and below. Moreover, the Edges are intersected by
several main highways connecting Sheffield and Chesterfield
with the cities, towns and villages of Derbyshire, and the best
known of them all is perhaps the A625 which descends to
Hathersage by way of Millstone Edge Nick. The famous
Surprise View is disclosed at this point and its name doubtless
arises from the sudden change of scene from the desolate
moors to the extensive panorama of the High Peak. And
curiously enough the road here is flanked by Millstone Edge
and Lawrencefield, both of which are in fact disused quarries
and nowadays deserted by all save the expert rock climber. To
sum up, these picturesque Edges are a series of geological
faults consisting of superb gritstone and all of them are
characterised by length and steepness.

All these Edges—E—are readily accessible from the
interesecting roads—R—, and from south to north are as
follows:

E	Chatsworth and Birchen's
R	Baslow to Chesterfield, A619
E	Gardom's
R	Baslow to Sheffield, A621
E	Baslow
R	Calver to A621
E	Curbar and Froggatt

Map 3
The Edges

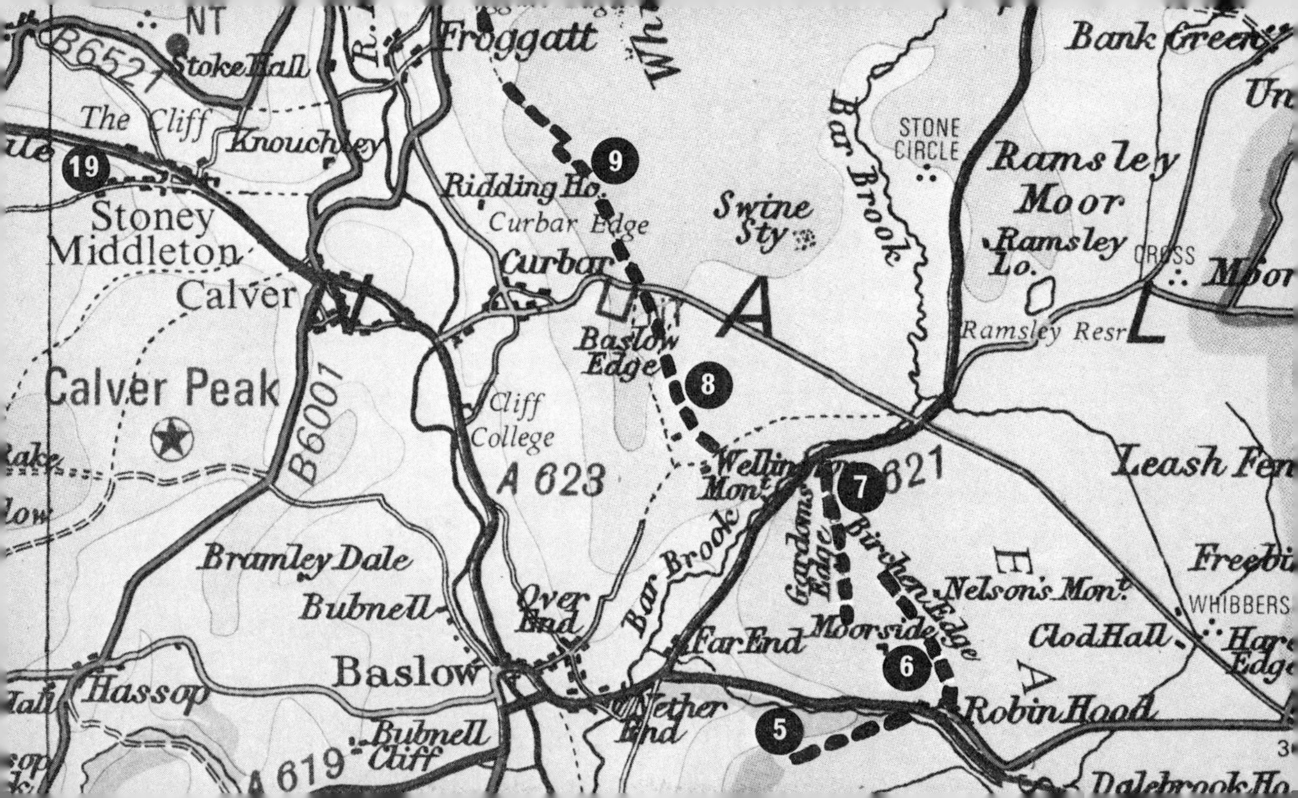
Froggatt
Bank Green
NT
Stoke Hall
B6521
The Cliff
Knouchley
STONE CIRCLE
Ramsley Moor
Ramsley Lo.
CROSS
Bar Brook
Ridding Ho.
Curbar Edge
Swine Sty
Stoney Middleton
Curbar
Calver
Ramsley Resr
Baslow Edge
Calver Peak
B6007
Cliff College
A 623
Leash Fen
Wellington Mon.t
Bar Brook
Bramley Dale
Gardoms Edge
Birchen Edge
Freebi
Bubnell
Over End
Nelson's Mon.t
WHIBBERS
Moorside
Far End
Clod Hall
Baslow
Hassop
Nether End
Robin Hood
Bubnell Cliff
A 619
Dalebrook Ho
19
9
8
7
6
5

R   Froggatt to Sheffield, B6054
R   Calver to Fox House, A6011
E   Lawrencefield
R   Hathersage to Fox House, A625—The Surprise View
E   Millstone, Carl Wark, Higger and Burbage
R   Hathersage to A625
E   Stanage
R   Bamford to Stanage
E   Bamford
R   Ladybower to Sheffield, A57
E   Derwent

Mountain photographers should note that as these Edges have a western aspect they are only well illuminated on a sunny afternoon. It is always advisable to go from south to north and if it is desired to include climbers in action the most propitious occasions are on fine weekends; they are usually deserted in mid-week.

Chatsworth Edge

This is the most southerley Edge overlooking the Derwent
Valley, and rises to the south of A619, less than half a mile
below the Robin Hood Inn. There is a large lay-by almost
opposite the rocks, with room for about a dozen cars, at the
end of which a locked gate gives access to a lane and bridge
over the stream. Immediately opposite stands the Sentinel
Rock with its immense overhang, where Don Whillans and
Joe Brown pioneered some of the most difficult crack climbs
of the 1950s. A level cart track goes to the R parallel with the
stream, and on the L appears first Emerald Buttress and then
Emperor Buttress higher up the hillside. Smaller crags are
distributed between the three and a sketchy track leads up to
the crest of the Edge at its terminus. There are over sixty routes
on Chatsworth Edge.

Route 5. Drive up the Chesterfield Road from Baslow and
park your car in the Lay-by on the R. Walk over to the crags
and turn R for the end of the Edge. Then make your way up
to its crest and bear L along the track, which after several ups
and downs eventually descends to the cart track near a gate,
well beyond the Sentinel Rock.

Plate 27 **Route 5** Chatsworth Edge, Sentinel Rock

Plate 28 **Route 5**— Emerald Buttress

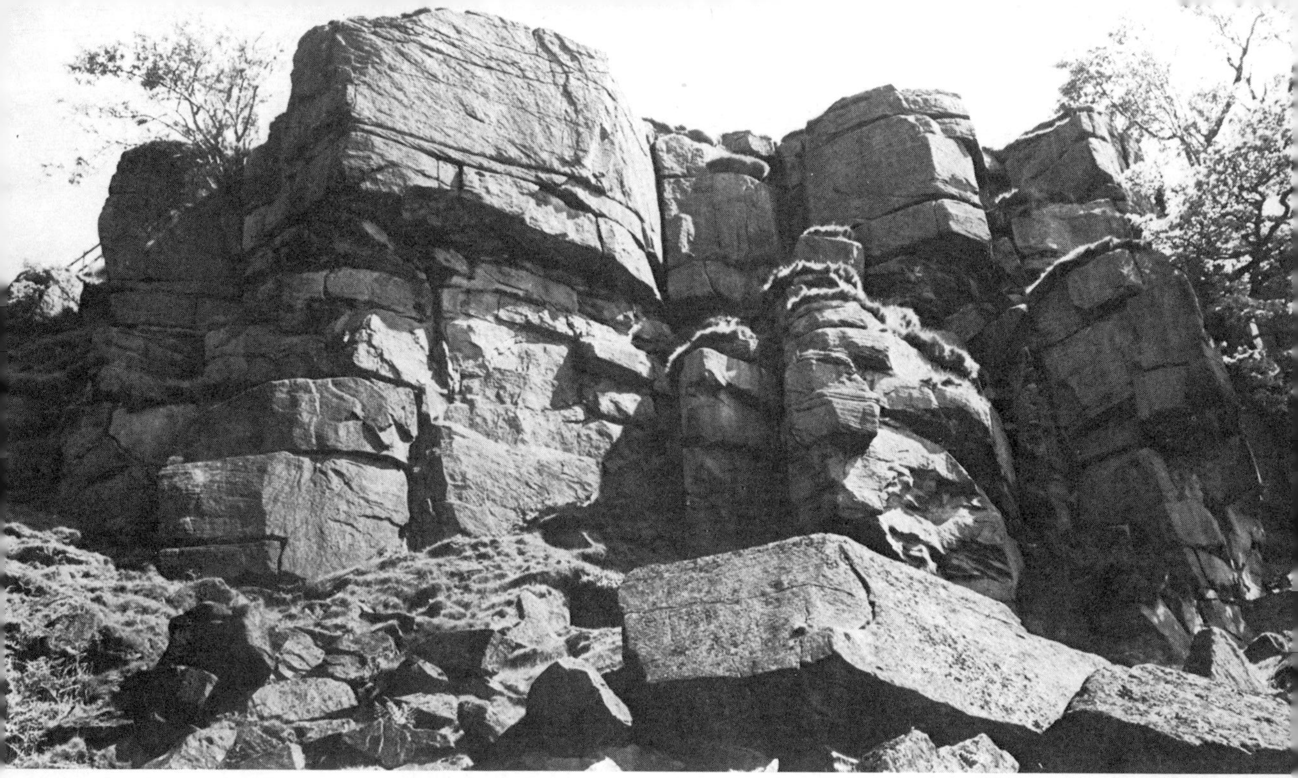

Plate 29 Route 5 – Emperor Buttress

Birchen's Edge

This Edge, crowned by Nelson's slender monument, lies to the north of Chatsworth Edge and extends for nearly a mile parallel with, and to the east of, Gardom's Edge. It is easily reached from the Robin Hood Inn by a well-trodden path which begins at a gate and stile, a few yards up B6050 from the inn. The Edge is much shattered until Copenhagen Wall is reached, whence the buttresses, some 50 feet high, are continuous to a point just beyond the Monument. A few yards behind the crest are three prominent boulders, named respectively from L to R, Victory, Reliance and Royal Soverin; they, together with the Nelson column and gritstone wall, are well seen from Gardom's on a sunny afternoon. The climbs are relatively short and steep, and all have nautical names.

Route 6. Drive to the Robin Hood Inn and leave your car in the commodious park, but since this is reserved for customers it is wise to take some refreshment before embarking upon this walk. Follow the path all the way to the Monument, and beyond it scale the grassy bank to the O.S. Station, then stroll back along the Edge, noting the features mentioned. When within sight of the inn, descend to the path and so back to your car.

Plate 30 **Route 6**—Climbing Copenhagen Wall

Victory | Reliance | Royal Soverin

Plate 31 **Route 6**— Three Boulders conspicuous from afar

Plate 22 Barrels of ... Nelson's Monument dominates the Edge...

Gardom's Edge

This Edge overlooks the Bar Brook Valley and is about a mile in length. It is characterised by numerous buttresses that jut out at almost regular intervals from a shattered front, but to clearly observe this feature it is necessary to walk up to Wellington's Monument which is exactly opposite on the other side of the valley. The southern extremity of the Edge may be reached by a short walk from the Robin Hood Inn on A619, but it is more often approached from A621 where its northern extremity overhangs the road.

Route 7. Drive up the walled A621 from Baslow and leave your car in a small bay below the Edge. This is the only safe parking place on this busy highway and there is just room for about four small cars. Climb the track on the L, cross the wire fence and walk to the southern end of the Edge where the immense boulders peter out, and from which point observe the view to the east of Birchen's Edge, crowned by Nelson's Monument. Now return and note the following: Blenheim Buttress, Apple Buttress, Grooved Wall, Bilberry Buttress, Prow Buttress, Marble Wall, Undertaker's Buttress, Gardom's Gate Buttress and Battlement Buttress.

The naming of the Buttress portrayed in plate 33 has romantic associations; for in the early '30s Eric Byne and his friend, Clifford Moyer, were cleaning out the crack when he found a lovely apple which he ate. He discovered it had been left there by a lady whom he met later and eventually married!

Arete ——— Crack

Plate 33 **Route 7**—Apple Buttress

Baslow Edge

This escarpment rises to the north-east of Baslow and is the southern continuation of Curbar, from which it is separated by the Gap that carries the road on to Big Moor. Its southern extremity is crowned by Wellington's Monument which frowns upon Bar Brook in the valley below, and on a sunny afternoon opens up the best prospect of Gardom's Edge in its entirety on the rim of the moor opposite. Baslow Edge is about a mile in length and its gritstone crags are much broken and display no continuous line of cliffs. But the moor behind it is decked with an immense obelisk that is conspicuous from afar and may be scaled at its western end as shown in the accompanying photograph. The routes on the Edge are short and not very difficult.

Route 8. Drive up the narrow, twisting road from Curbar and park your car in the space on the L, a little distance beyond the Gap. Walk back along the road and cross the stile on the L, which gives you access to a grassy cart track that keeps some distance away from the Edge. Stroll along this pleasant promenade and make for the obelisk of the Eagle Stone, then take a direct line for Wellington's Monument for the spacious views unfolded round the southern arc. Return along the Edge and so back to your car.

Plate 24 Route 8 — Curbar Edge from Baslow Edge

Plate 35 **Route 8**– A Climb on the adjacent moor: Eagle Stone

Plate 36 **Route 8**—Wellington's Monument

Curbar Edge

This escarpment frowns upon the village of Curbar from
which it takes its name. A steep road rises from the cottages
and passes on to the Big Moor behind it through a gap that
separates this Edge from Baslow Edge to the south. It is about
a mile in length and terminates in the north with Beech
Buttress, the point of separation from Froggatt Edge which
swings round to the north-east above B6054. Curbar Edge is
noted for its crack climbs, and for some very hard modern face
routes.

Route 9. Drive up from Curbar, or if you come from
Gardom's Edge continue along A621 and take the first L turn
which later passes through the gap in the escarpment and
bends to the R where several parking places are just off the
road, immediately below Curbar Edge. Ascend one of the
tracks to attain the path on top of it and while walking
northwards note the Great Buttress with its ferocious cracks
and walls, and half a mile beyond it, the Amphitheatre with
Beech Buttress to the north.

Plate 37 **Route 9**—The Great Buttress

Froggatt Edge

This is named after the hamlet immediately below and is about a mile in length. It may be attained from the Chequers Inn on B6054, or more conveniently higher up where a gate on the R gives direct access to the Edge at a point where the road begins to cross the moor. A grassy cart road runs along the top of this escarpment and continues above Curbar Edge. It is advisable to park the vehicle in a recess near the gate or in a large car-park 150 yards to the north. Froggatt Edge is scenically superior to the Edges already described, and its highest elevation rises the Pinnacle, a square gritstone tower separated from the adjacent Edge by a deep gully; it is fifty five feet high and a conspicuous object when seen from below.

Route 10. Drive up B6054 from Calver and park your car near the gate. Walk along the cart track for about a mile, or for some 200 yards beyond the highest point of the Edge. Then descend the track on the R which leads to the base of the cliffs and walk northwards, noting the sharp corner of Green Gut, with Brown's Eliminate just beyond it. The Pinnacle now appears ahead, with behind it the steep Three Pebble Slab. Retrace your steps to the top of the cliffs and again walk northwards to observe more closely the upper section of the Pinnacle and the strange projecting pinnacle on the other side of it, with near at hand some vertical slabs supporting a collection of horizontal rocks below which are Swimmers' Chimney and Holly Groove.

Crack

Plate 38 **Route 10**—Solomon's Crack and Chequer's Buttress

Brown's Eliminate   Green Gut

Plate 39 **Route 10**—Two tough climbs

Plate 40 **Route 10**—The Pinnacle from below

Plate 41 **Route 10**—Three Pebble Slab

Plate 42 **Route 10**—Close-up of the pinnacle

Plate 43 **Route 10**—The Leaning Pinnacle

Holly Groove

Swimmers' Chimney

Plate 44 **Route 10**—Groove and Chimney climbs with Froggatt Cave below, and Whillans Cave Wall

Lawrencefield

This is a small quarry immediately to the south of the Surprise View, but it is unseen until it is discovered. Characterised by a dirty pool at the base of the vertical cliffs, it is hidden by a copse of scattered trees on the west and on this account its photography is difficult unless a 28mm wide-angle lens is available. It may be reached by a grassy path from the top of the Surprise, or by a rough track which begins on the other side of the L wall of Millstone Edge Nick. A wire fence runs round the top of the quarry to prevent sheep falling into the pool, and this is crossed lower down to reach a corner which reveals the picturesque gritstone outcrop on the L.

Route 11. Drive up to the Surprise View from Hathersage and park your car either in a recess below Millstone Edge Nick or in a large car park on the L of the road crossing the moor. Walk down to the quarry and note the Great Wall above the pool, split by two cracks known as Boulevard and High Street which are scarred by pitons and reached from the Great Shelf. Excalibur goes up the right corner and further to the R lies Gingerbread Slab on which are six tricky routes. Three Tree Climb, Great Harry and Pulpit Groove are on the more broken wall on the L of the pool, and Suspense takes the wall falling into it.

Plate 45 **Route 11**—The North Wall

Plate 46 **Route 11** — First Glimpse of the quarry

Boulevard | High Street | Excalibur | Gingerbread Slab

Plate 47 **Route 11** —Frontal view of the Great Wall and Pool

Millstone Edge

Anyone who drives up from Hathersage to the Surprise is bound to be impressed by the great rock barrier that crowns the horizon on the L. This conspicuous Edge was once an immense quarry and it assumes its most spectacular aspect on a sunny afternoon. The shadows then cast by the sharp corners of this vertical wall of gritstone outline the succession of Bays which are the preserve of modern free climbing. As will be seen when the quarry is entered by the cart track from the Surprise, a spoil heap lies at the corner of each bay and most of them have become overgrown with vegetation since the quarry was abandoned. This characteristic feature means that a party of climbers may be scaling the cliffs of one bay and be quite unaware of another party in the next. The track emerges opposite a gigantic slab known as the Embankment, which is scarred by the innumerable pitons that have been driven into its three almost parallel cracks. Such aid climbing has long since ceased.

Route 12. You may reach Millstone Edge as described in the last monograph, and although it is possible to drive right up to it the rough surface of the cart track will deter you if you have any respect for your car. And while you may walk some distance along it, it is better to keep nearer to each bay if you wish to inspect the climbing routes more clearly. Of the many that are well marked, the following are the most important: London Wall, the Embankment Route including Time for Tea and Scritto's Republic, Lyons Corner House, Covent Garden, Lambeth Chimney and the Great Slab.

Plate 48 The Surprise View

Plate 49 Millstone Edge from A625

Plate 60. Route 12. The Embankment.

Plate 51 **Route 12**—London Wall and the Bond Street section

PLATE 68 Part 12. Broken-up beds of fine-grained Embankment (Grey) North Reed area)

Carl Wark

This ancient fortress forms a prominent outcrop of gritstone
in the valley threaded by Burbage Brook: it is hemmed in on
the east by the long line of Burbage Rocks; on the north-west
by the loftier Higger Tor and on the south-west by the
swelling moorland that terminates abruptly in Millstone Edge.
Its crest slopes up from west to east to end in a conspicuous
Prow, and is supported on either side by shattered crags and
boulders. These merge with the moor in the west where the
primitive fortifications can still be seen. Carl Wark may be
observed to advantage from the southern end of Burbage
Rocks, whence a path leads almost straight up to the Prow,
but it can also be reached from any side by one or other of the
many tracks through the bracken.

Route 13. Drive up from Hathersage, or down from the Fox
House Inn, and park your car off the road in the space above
the bridge over Burbage Brook. Follow the cart track to a
locked gate and bear L along a path that drops downhill to
the Brook where care is necessary if the stream is crossed by
the large boulders. Then walk up the grassy path towards the
Prow and scramble up the broken crags on its L. Stroll round
the rim of the fortress and observe the fine elevation of Higger
Tor, noting also the fortifications and the water trough near
the sheepfold at its south-western corner. Then either continue
your walk as described in Route 14, or return direct to
your car.

Plate 53 **Route 13**—The approach to Carl Wark

Plate 54 **Route 13**—Boulders defending the Fortress

Leaning Tower | Hole in Slabs

Plate 55 Route 12 Higsar Tor from the Brow of the fort

Higger Tor

This escarpment tops the hill behind Millstone Edge and lies to the R of the narrow road rising to the L below the Surprise. It is relatively small and much shattered, but is characterised by a tremendous leaning tower, on which the Rasp is one of its toughest climbs.

Route 14. Park your car on the wide grass verge below the Tor and walk along the crest of the Edge to take a closer look at the tower. That this escarpment is less popular than its neighbours is evident by the absence of any clearly marked track through the sea of boulders at its base. The spacious views round the western arc are magnificent.

Higger Tor attains the 1,400 feet contour and can be the culminating point of a magnificent walk, which should be started from the vicinity of the Bridge over Burbage Brook. Park your car in the large bay above the stream and follow the cart track to the locked gate. Bear L and pick up the path which takes a direct line for Carl Wark, a prominent feature on the moor ahead. This leads to the rocky Prow of the Hill Fort whose summit may be attained by a nice scramble, and then continue round the northern perimeter to the walled defences at its western end. Now follow the path to Higger Tor on the far horizon, to the L of which the Leaning Tower is prominent, as also a conspicuous hole in the piled up slabs of gritstone in the centre of the escarpment. Examine this gigantic jumble of rocks and then turn R to descend over the moor in the direction of Burbage Rocks; on reaching them bear R and keep to the Edge through the quarry and so back to your car.

Plate 56 **Route 14**—The Leaning Tower

Burbage Edge

Known also as Burbage Rocks, this conspicuous Edge
consists of a long stretch of straggling buttresses and large
boulders, and is divided into two well-defined sections, each
about a mile in length. That to the north lies across the valley
to the north-east of Higger Tor, while that to the south faces
Carl Wark. Regarded by some climbers as the southern
extension of Stanage Edge, its northern extremity is most
easily reached from the old Sheffield Road, beside which lies a
commodious car park. Paths run along the top of the Edge
and through the heather and boulders at its base. The less
popular southern section may be attained from A625 at the
point where a bridge spans Burbage Brook, about half a mile
from Fox House Inn. Burbage is a good training ground for
the tyro because its cracks and chimneys are at a relatively
easy gradient. Some of the best-known courses are Mutiny,
Amazon, Hollyash and Curving Cracks, but there are also
many modern hard problems.

Route 15. Drive up the old Sheffield Road from Hathersage
and park your car near the terminal rocks of the Edge.
Descend to the path at its base and walk south for about a
mile, then return along its loftier crest. Afternoon light is best
for its photography.

Plate 57 **Route 15**—Ash Tree Wall

Stanage Edge

This magnificent escarpment consists of superb gritstone and extends northwards from the Cowper Stone for some four miles to form the western lip of Hallam Moor; it is about five miles from Sheffield. A narrow road, suitable for motor cars, runs uphill from Hathersage and swings round to the L to descend eventually to Bamford. From this road numerous paths rise through the heather and bracken and during the approach to the Edge its long line of serrated crags are seen to extend along the skyline; on a favourable afternoon they gleam like gold in the westering sunlight.

The cliffs vary in height from twenty to eighty feet, but average about sixty feet: the lowest section of the excarpment is at its northern extremity, between High Neb and Stanage End. The Edge displays several breaks throughout its entire length, but the most conspicuous is that which carries the old Roman Road, from the reservoirs by way of Long Causeway down into the valley in the direction of Hathersage. The rock staircase in the gap is familiarly known as Jacob's Ladder.

Stanage Edge is roughly divided into six separate outcrops, and from south to north are as follows: Black Hawk terminating at the Flying Buttress; Robin Hood with its Balcony of caves; Intermediate; Wall End from the Plantation to Jacob's Ladder; High Neb which dominates the line of cliffs and Stanage End. It would be risky to attempt to give an exact figure for the number of well-known climbs, but it is safe to say they probably tot up to towards 900. Many of the fine buttresses have vertical faces and are seamed with routes to suit the powers of every rock climber.

Should you wish to explore Stanage Edge in its entirety it is necessary to have the guide-book if each and every route is to be located with certainty. To mention only a few I give the following which are so popular that you may have to queue before your turn comes to tackle the chosen climb. Black Hawk Area: Mantelpiece Buttress, Grotto Slab, B.H.

Traverse L, B.H. Hell Crack, B.H. Slit, Anatomy, Manchester Buttress, the Dangler and the Unprintable. Robin Hood Area: Inverted V and Mississippi Buttress. Intermediate Group: the Unconquerables. Wall End: Goliath's Grove. High Neb: Old Friends, Quietus, Inaccessible Crack, Twisting Crack and Overhanging Chimney. Stanage End: Surgeon's Saunter and Green Streak.

Route 16. Drive up the old Sheffield Road from Hathersage and at the fork take the R branch; park your car on the grass verge below the Cowper Stone. Ascend one of the paths through the boulders and on attaining the crest of the cliffs turn L and walk at least as far as High Neb. Then descend to the base of the escarpment and walk back along the undulating path past all the towers and buttresses, noting the technique of the climbers in action. On a sunny afternoon this is one of the most exhilarating and enchanting excursions in the Peak and by many regarded as the crowning glory of the district.

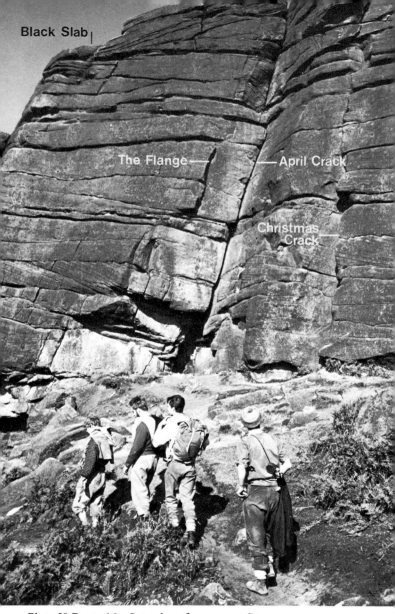

Black Slab

The Flange — — April Crack

Christmas Crack

Plate 58 **Route 16**—Saturday afternoon at Stanage

Plate 59 **Route 16**—The Cowper Stone

Plate 60 **Route 16**—Black Hawk area

Plate 61 **Route 16**— Black Hawk traverse left, and Slit

Plate 62 **Route 16**—The Flying Buttress

Inverted V

R-Hand Buttress
Direct

Plate 63 **Route 16**—Two famous climbs

Plate 64 **Route 16**—Robin Hood's Wall with Desperation
below and Cave Eliminate to the left

Green Crack

Black Slab

Plate 65 **Route 16**—Robin Hood area

Plate 66 **Route 16**—Caves on Robin Hood's Balcony

High Neb

Plate 67 **Route 16**—High Neb from Jacob's Ladder

Plate 68 **Route 16**—Close-up of High Neb with the roof of Quietus and the wall of Old Friends on the right

Bamford Edge

This lofty escarpment frowns upon the Ladybower Dam, and is situated on the private property of the Water Board. The Edge is some two miles long and characterised by a number of bold buttresses, interspersed with boulder-strewn slopes. A derelict building stands inside the wire fence, whence a narrow track rises through the heather and bracken to a break in the crags. On reaching the gap it swings round to the L, past an abandoned millstone in the making, and continues thence along the crest of the main cliffs with spacious views of the dam and reservoir. There are a number of climbs on the buttresses. A narrow road leaves the highway about half a mile below the Dam, and after passing through a beautiful avenue of trees it sweeps up the slopes of the moor, passes round the southern end of the Edge and, at Dennis Knoll, turns R for Stanage. There is space for only one car on the side of the road opposite the derelict building.

Route 17. Drive to Bamford and continue towards the reservoir, then turn up the first road on the R. Park your car in the only available space below the escarpment, cross the fence and walk up to the Edge. Continue along its crest until you reach the last buttress portrayed in plate 71, and after admiring the extensive panorama return to your car.

Plate 69 **Route 17**—Ladybower dam from the last buttress

Derwent Edge

This is the last and most northerly of the eastern barriers of the Peak District and frowns upon the blue waters of Ladybower and Derwent Reservoirs far below. It differs from the Edges already described in that it exhibits no continuous façade of gritstone, but is notable for the strange outcrops of rock which stand in splendid isolation upon the very edge of the moor. Their naked elevation in this otherwise bare stretch of country raises a geological problem which is intrinsically more wonderful than boulders transported by the Ice Age glaciers.

Access to Derwent Edge is possible from almost every side and a well trodden path runs along the crest of the ridge as far as Back Tor, but since it is preserved ground it should be avoided during the shooting season.

Of all the walks in the Peak District, I think it would be true to say that Derwent Edge is the finest and most picturesque, because it not only displays the above mentioned collection of rocks to perfection, but is high enough to reveal a panorama that delights the eye from start to finish of its four miles from Cutthroat Bridge to Back Tor at its northern extremity.

Route 18. The best starting point for motorists is Cutthroat Bridge on the A57, about a mile to the east of Ladybower Reservoir, where ample parking space will be found on either side of the river. Highshaw Clough descends to this point from the north and a path leads up to a gate on the L of the stream. The track rises gently and soon bears due west across the lower stretches of the moor which is dappled with purple heather whence an occasional grouse rises and calls you to Go-Back, Go-Back. On reaching the highest point of the path it joins the one coming up from Ashopton and turns R to ascend the steep slopes of Whinstone Lee Tor which opens up a fine prospect of Ladybower and Derwent Reservoirs. Leaving behind the many boulders, the path goes to the R to the Huckling Stones and thence L in a direct line for the Wheel Stones on the far horizon, perhaps the most remarkable

Plate 70 **Route 18**—Derwent Reservoir from Whinstone Lee Tor

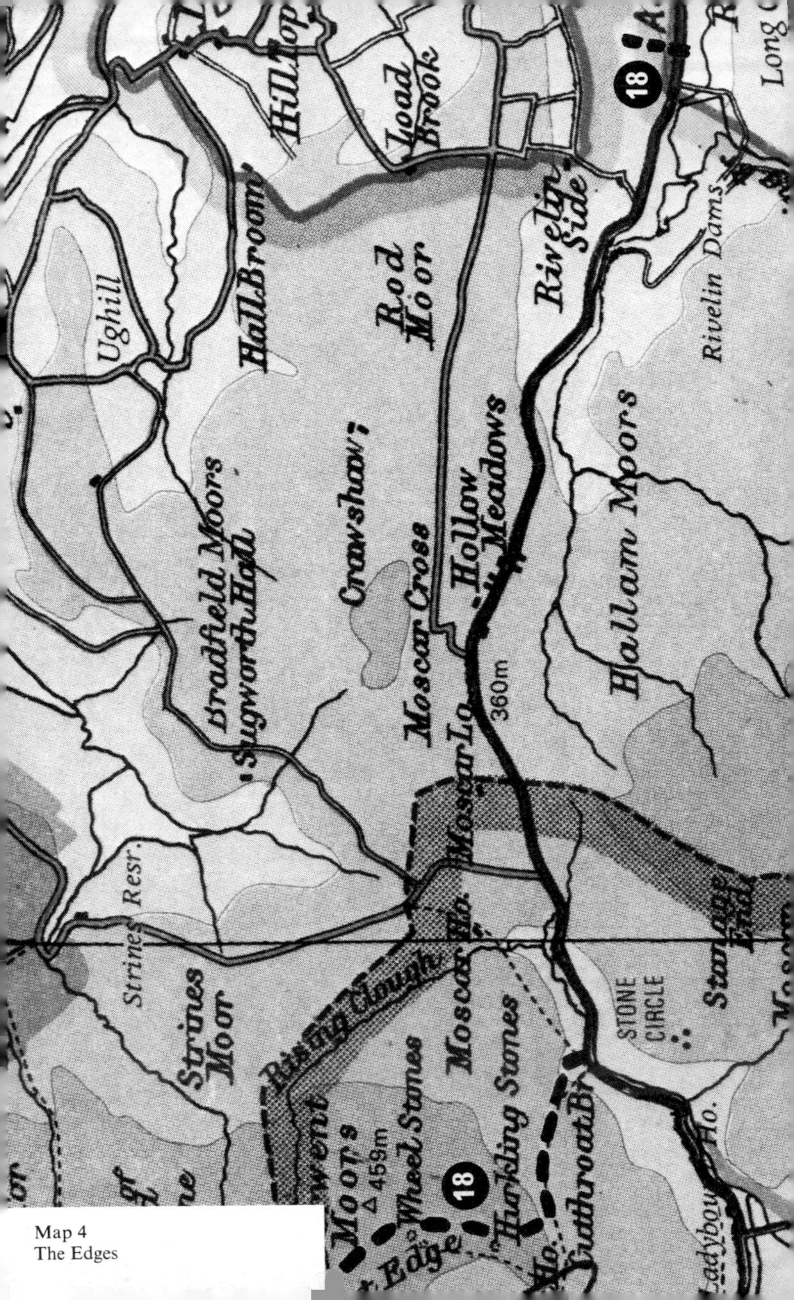

Map 4
The Edges

16
Moor
Stanedge
Lo.
Redmires
Resrs.
17
A 6013
Stanage Pole
Rud
Hill
Quarries
Green's Ho
Bamford
Edge
16
Ox
Stones
419
Brookfield
Manor
18
BAMFORD STA
Kimber
Co.
Burbage
Rocks
15
Carhead
The Tower
Garner Ho.
Toothill
Burbage
Moor
A 625
Edge
Hathersage
Broadhay
Offerton Hall
Moor
STA
Nether
Hall
Callow Ho.
Parsons Ho.
Millstone
Dinge Brook

collection of rocks on this Edge. Cross the Moscar House path to reach them and then continue to the prominent crags of White Tor. Climb the path on their R and go ahead to the next collection of rocks. And it is here that you must keep a sharp lookout for the famous Salt Cellar because this obelisk stands on the L below the crest of the ridge and can easily be missed. On a clear day it is a magnificent viewpoint, not only for the appraisal of Howden Moor to the north but also for the bleak uplands of Kinder and Bleaklow to the west. Many walkers go no further but it is worth while for the enthusiast to continue along the ridge to Dovestones Tor which is the next outcrop and an occasional resort of the rock climber. The track passes to the R and shortly reveals still further to the R the strangely named Cakes of Bread. It then falls gently to a stretch of marshy ground before rising to Bradfield Gate Head where a pointer directs the walker to the R for Strines. Ahead rise the prominent rocks of Back Tor surmounted by an OS Triangulation Station, beyond which the moor falls away to the north. This lofty viewpoint discloses a splendid panorama of the characteristic Peak District moorland and includes a clear view of the two mile long ridge that dominates Bleaklow.

RIVELIN EDGE rises to the north of A57, and as it is only four miles to the east of Cutthroat Bridge it may be visited conveniently after the descent from Derwent Edge. It is the much quarried outcrop of gritstone opposite the Dams and nearby Norfolk Arms, but its real attraction lies in the conspicuous Rivelin Needle, which was first climbed in 1932 by Eric Byne of the Sheffield Climbing Club. To reach it, high up on the face of the cliffs, park your car in the space on the L of the busy highway almost opposite the Dams, whence follow the well-trodden path through the heather. On leaving the level moor, take every care while ascending the steep ground which is strewn with large boulders, and to facilitate progress keep to the sketchy track which finally emerges immediately below the Needle.

Plate 71 **Route 18**—The Wheel Stones

Plate 72 **Route 18**—White Tor

Plate 73 **Route 18**—The Salt Cellar

Plate 74 **Route 18**— The strangely named Cakes of Bread

Plate 75 **Route 18** — Back Tor

Stoney Middleton

The A623 connects Chapel-en-le-Frith with Calver and
Baslow in the Derwent Valley and its most spectacular section
is Middleton Dale near its eastern terminus. Here the twisting
road descends gradually through a narrow ravine which is
hemmed in on the south by a series of limestone quarries
whose emerging grey-white dust mars the vivid green of the
prolific vegetation, and on the north by a long line of
stupendous vertical limestone cliffs that terminate abruptly at
the little village of Stoney Middleton. These lofty crags
overhang the highway, but are seldom seen by the passing
motorist owing to the dense belt of trees that flanks the steep
grassy bank beside the road. To obtain the clearest possible
conception of their grandeur it is necessary to walk along the
crest of the ridge enclosing the south side of the dale, but even
so the trees are so prolific that they mar what could be one of
the grandest prospects in the Peak.

Photographers will soon discover the problems involved in
taking close-ups of climbers on these crags owing to the
encroaching trees, but the difficulty may be overcome by using
a telephoto lens from the higher reaches of the road in the
large quarry opposite.

Beneath this dynamic collection of buttress, gully and bay
runs a cart track, known to climbers as the South promenade.
During fine weekends it affords an admirable site for campers
as it is well hidden from the road below and gives immediate
access to the ledges and caves, and to many of the routes
festooning the cliffs. It terminates abruptly at the Prayer
Wheel Wall, to the R of which rises Minestrone, one of the
many very severe ascents on this limestone wall. Nearby
Fingal's Cave is conspicuous, and to the L of it rise Horizon
and Aux Bicyclettes, two less difficult ascents, while to the R
rise White Knight and the Pearly Gates which are a greater
test of the powers of the rock climber. Routes of great interest
and difficulty abound here, with 217 separate climbs on the
main cliff. There is a tremendous cluster of climbs on

Windyledge Buttress, which is approached by a fine exposed rock shelf to the Keyhole Cave. Great classics of hard climbing from several generations co-exist at Stoney Middleton, with Frank Elliott's Aurora (1933), R. Moseley's Sin (1952), B. Webb's Mortuary Steps (1961) and Tom Proctor's Our Father (1967). All in all, Stoney Middleton is the most popular and best developed limestone escarpment in Derbyshire.

Route 19. If you are staying anywhere in the Derwent Valley, drive to Calver and then through the trees to Stoney Middleton. There is a petrol station beyond the village that is situated beneath the first buttress of the long line of cliffs, and park your car in the space opposite. Then walk up through one the quarries on the south side of the dale for the general view of the immense wall of crags, and later descend to the South Promenade for a close view of their ledges, caves and the various courses festooning the wall overhead.

See map, page 93

Plate 76 **Route 19** — The long line of limestone cliffs

Plate 77 **Route 19**—Fingal's Cave

Plate 78 **Route 19**—Aurora from the road

Plate 79 **Route 19** — Three favourite climbs; Windyledge Buttress and the Tower of Babel

Plate 80 **Route 19**—Windhover and Aurora. Note the climbers on the Terrace and Windhover

Lathkill Dale

This beautiful valley is situated to the south of Bakewell and to the west of Rowsley. It extends for about five miles from Alport in the direction of Monyash but peters out in the fields just short of the village. The first section runs north-west as far as Conksbury Bridge and is shallow but well wooded on its northern slopes. It then bends due west and narrows considerably, its steeper banks on either side being well shagged with woods, which on the north fall to a wide band of green sward beside the stream. The narrowest section of the dale begins below the village of Over Haddon and here the trees descend right down to the very edge of the Lathkill, but terminate abruptly about a mile further up the valley. The limestone of the district thereafter makes its appearance and several outcrops project through the grass on the hillsides. Later the dale bifurcates; the L branch is known as Cales Dale, and the R as Ricklow Dale. The latter attains very narrow proportions and after passing through a splendid little limestone gorge, widens out into the undulating country near Monyash.

The Lathkill is one of the loveliest rivers in the peak and displays a wealth of little weirs, whose water-play adds so much to the charm of the walk through the dale. Like many streams in the limestone district, it disappears in places and runs below ground. It first sees the light of day in a hole in the side of Ricklow Dale, but very little water appears in its bed until near Over Haddon. The fishing is private and the delight of any angler who is lucky enough to obtain permission to use it.

Map 5
The Lathkill

Route 20. Alport is the usual starting point for this enchanting walk and if you go there by car and have no one to drive it to Monyash it is just too bad. The alternative is to park the vehicle at Alport and walk to Monyash and back, a distance of about ten miles. From Alport Bridge follow the path of the L of the placid stream and on reaching the road cross Conksbury Bridge Then take the path through the trees on the R of the river, which soon emerges from its leafy canopy, and continue thence along the broad stretch of green sward as far as the cottages, with views high up on the R of Over Haddon. Now enter the forest beyond, with its silent pools and the soft murmur of its foliage, which will transport you to the very threshold of Arcady. On leaving this woodland glade the dale becomes more commonplace, with no plash of water to charm your ear and little but limestone and grass to delight your eye. Continue ahead through the winding dale, past Cales Dale on the L, and beyond it on the L observe the hole in the limestone through which emerges the infant stream in dry weather, then round the next bend and look into the hole in Ricklow Dale where in wet weather the stream issues from the limestone. Pass through the narrow gorge and then keep to the path across the fields to Monyash.

Motorists who desire to see only the most picturesque section of Lathkill Dale may drive south from Bakewell and park their cars near Conksbury Bridge, whence it is about a mile to Over Haddon.

Plate 81 **Route 20**—Conksbury Bridge

Plate 82 **Route 20**—Angler's paradise

Plate 83 **Route 20**—Forest murmurs in Lathkill's Arcady

The Wye

This beautiful river flows through a succession of narrow
limestone dales which afford some of the loveliest scenery in
the Peak. It rises in the dim recesses of Poole's Cavern in
Buxton and on emerging from its underground course is
utilised for decorative and industrial purposes, whence the
stream is allowed to follow its natural course. The valleys
threaded by the Wye are Ashwood Dale, Wye Dale, Chee
Dale, Miller's Dale and Monsal Dale. Thenceforward it
meanders through the tree-girt meadows in the vicinity of
Ashford, Bakewell and Haddon, finally to be received by the
Derwent at Rowsley. The river is some sixteen miles in length,
but the first ten miles are cut so deeply into the limestone and
its enclosing slopes are so steep that when the moors to the
north are observed from the lofty village of Taddington there
is no visual indication of its course.

Travellers who went by rail from Derby to Buxton or
Manchester before the line was closed will have glanced out of
the carriage window and seen its glittering surface as the train
sped in and out of the numerous tunnels which penetrate the
entire length of Monsal, Miller's and Chee Dales. Those who
like beautiful valley scenery will have been intrigued by these
scanty glimpses, and at the first opportunity will have
tramped the three dales from end to end as the only way of
discovering their hidden charms. And while those who stay in
either Bakewell or Buxton may go by car to one end or the
other, it is a distinct advantage to use the bus service between
the two towns as a convenient approach to the entrance to
Monsal Dale at one end and to return from Topley Pike at
the other. Pedestrians who are interested in photography will
find it best to walk up these three dales rather than down;
because not only is the water play on the river viewed to
greater advantage, but the sunlight illuminates the first two
dales better in the morning and Chee Dale cannot be
portrayed effectively until the late afternoon.

Until recent years these dales have been the strict preserve of the walker, who has revelled in the sylvan beauty of the changing scenery and perhaps lingered here and there to admire the precipitous outcrops of limestone which make their appearance in Miller's and Chee Dales. But since the development of this type of cliff as the play-ground of the rock climber, these sportsmen have explored each and every outcrop so thoroughly that routes of all grades of difficulty have been worked out. At the time of writing Raven Tor, Miller's Dale has become the major attraction, along with those outcrops on either side of the widening Wye below Litton Mill now known to climbers as Water-cum-Jolly.

Route 21. When Monsal Dale is approached from Bakewell, it is worth while to halt awhile at Ashford if only to observe its beautiful bridge spanning the River Wye, which has been the subject of many an artist and photographer. Some two miles further along the road the dale opens up on the R, whence you should tread the path on the western banks of the stream. The craggy slopes of Fin Cop rise on the R and wood shagged declivities enclose the valley on the L. The dale soon sweeps round to the R to disclose the great railway viaduct at the mouth of Longstone Tunnel, and after passing below it the valley bends sharply to the L but this section is seen at its finest from Monsal Head, immediately above the bend at Little Longstone. The path in the dale leads to a small bridge which gives access to the road on the R. Now walk ahead to Cressbrook Mill which stands at the entrance to Miller's Dale. Here the river once occupied the whole valley floor, but a dam failure has drained the lake. On the way to Litton Mill note the tree-clad cliffs of Water-cum-Jolly in which, from L to R, the outcrops are named Rubicon Wall, Axe Edge, Everglades, Psyche and Cupid. Pass through the mill and continue beside the river, noting at the next bend to the R the stupendous overhanging wall of limestone known as Raven Tor. This is about 170 feet high, with a cave at its base and overhang of 30 feet. Twenty-seven free climbs, protected by pitons and bolts, now seam this impregnable-looking abyss. They are

Map 6
The Wye

among the hardest in Britain and are test-pieces for rock experts from all over the world. A short walk leads to the main highway, near the Angler's Rest, where you proceed below Miller's Dale Station and turn R beyond the Dale Hotel to enter Chee Dale by a path on the L which rises steeply to reach the abandoned railway.

Continue ahead and before reaching the tunnel turn R by a wall where the grassy path goes downhill to the stream. Some distance ahead the slopes on the L of the valley increase in steepness and ultimately give place to the sheer limestone precipices of Chee Tor. Here the path divides, but it is better to follow the L branch beside the river. On and on you go, crossing a bridge to the north side of the stream, where you soon encounter the Stepping Stones below an overhanging crag. In wet weather you may get your feet wet, but you will soon forget any discomfort when you reach the grand array of limestone pinnacles and buttresses on the L, which mark the terminus of this spectacular dale. To reach Topley Pike, you cross the footbridge near some cottages and walk up the road through a copse to the main road where you may catch your bus to the desired destination. The whole course of the River Wye is the delight of the angler, but the fishing is either private or preserved by associations or hotels.

The Monsal Trail was created in 1980 when the Peak Planning Board took over most of the former Midland Railway track through the Wye Valley. And while it roughly keeps to Route 21, diversions are necessary owing to the closed tunnels at Little Longstone, between Cressbrook Mill and Litton Mills, and between Miller's Dale and Chee Dale, where in the two latter sections the path beside the river must be followed. This elevated trail opens up charming views of the valley but much of the walk from Monsal Head is enclosed by high trees.

Plate 84 Ashford bridge

Fin Cop

Plate 25 Route 21 Lower reaches of Monsal Dale

Plate 86 **Route 21** — The Dale from Monsale Head

Plate 87 **Route 21** — Raven Tor, with some of the hardest free climbs in Britain

Plate 88 **Route 21**—Chee Tor, another 'super severe' cliff

Plate 23 Baie de Thal, and Col du Pelat, with the magnificent Plana Derruces

Shining Tor and the Goyt Valley

This eminence is the usual objective in the pleasant walk up the Goyt Valley, but its summit is more often attained by a direct approach from the Cat and Fiddle. This famous inn stands on the highest point of the Buxton-Macclesfield Road, but as there is a difference in altitude of a mere 143 feet, Shining Tor displays insufficient form or elevation to draw the climber. To the east and south its grassy flanks slope down gradually, to the north its broad ridge declines slightly to Cats Tor, while to the west it is more shattered near the summit and exposes a few rocks which improve its character. As a viewpoint it is disappointing because it is situated too far away from the valleys effectively to command them. But it has one saving feature in that its southern prospect is dominated by the graceful lines of distant Shutlingsloe.

Route 22. Drive up to the Cat and Fiddle and park your car near the inn. Walk a little way downhill in the direction of Macclesfield and bear R along a well worn cart track. This rises at an easy gradient and at the point where it bends to the R along the crest of Stake Side there is a splendid view of Shining Tor. Now follow the stone wall until a break appears exactly opposite your objective and then turn sharp L across the valley and walk up beside the stone wall to the O.S. station on its summit. This makes a pleasant afternoon stroll that could well follow a morning spent in the adjacent Goyt Valley.

The Goyt Valley has been formed by the erosion of its river which rises on Axe Edge Moor near the Cat and Fiddle. For the first four miles of its course it makes sweet music as it flows over the folded rocks of Millstone Grit, finally to lose its charm on entering Errwood Reservoir and later Fernilee Reservoir. The most beautiful part of this lovely valley is its southern section, from Goytsclough Quarry to Derbyshire Bridge on the old Macclesfield road, where the stream is hemmed in by picturesque moorland slopes which make a colourful tapestry that appeals to both artist and photographer.

The valley is threaded by a single track road, and since it is only three miles from Buxton it attracts an immense number of motorists whose movements are controlled by a one way system on certain days of the week, as clearly indicated by prominent notice boards. To reach it by car you leave Buxton by A5002 and at the top of Long Hill you turn L into Goyt Lane which descends in spacious curves, finally to pass over Errwood Dam. Here you turn L and drive along its western bank past Errwood Car Park, then through extensive woodlands and eventually emerge from their leafy canopy on open moorland at Goytsclough Quarry. Although the road continues beside the Goyt River, it is best to park your car here and walk all the way to Derbyshire Bridge, and on your return later drive slowly over the same section. Visitors who do not wish to make the complete tour could drive up A537 from Buxton and turn R before reaching the Cat and Fiddle. This two way road terminates at Derbyshire Bridge from which point the same walk could be undertaken in the opposite direction. There is also a fine circuit, descending the valley from the Cat and Fiddle and returning via Errwood Hall.

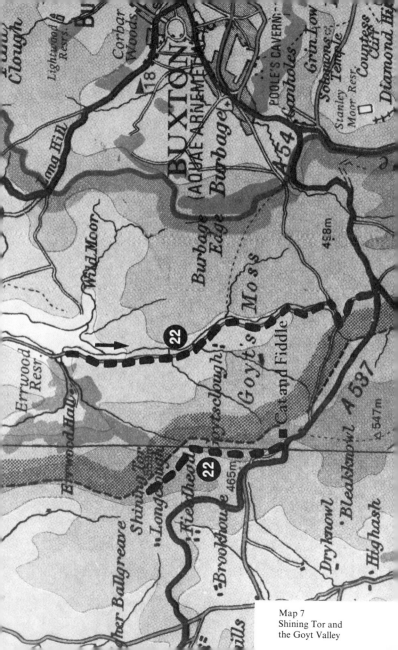

Map 7
Shining Tor and
the Goyt Valley

Plate 90 Shining Tor from the Cat and Fiddle

Plate 91 **Route 22**—Shining Tor from the cart track

Plate 22   The Goyt Valley with Goytsclough quarry on left

Plate 93 **Route 22**—Goyts Bridge

P. Ho...
Oakse... Hall
Newt...
Pyeclough
Merril Grove
Badger's Croft
Fleet Green
L.t Fleetgreen
...ngton Low
DANGER

Barley Hall
Morridge
Folly
Swainsmoor
489

Gib Tor
470m
Royal Cottage
...shaw ...cks
DANGER ZONE
Strines

A 53

23

Goldsitch Moss
Goldsitch Ho.
Hazel Barrow
Swythen Hill
Newchurch
Findlay
...r Cliffs

25
Hen Cloud
24
...ourn
Upper Hulme
...dle

Brook
Roachend
The Roaches
Greenlane
Windygates
Meerbrook

Clough Head
403m
Brownsett
Reach Grange
Lapwing Hall
Alder Lee

...dge
...er's Pool
...y Top
...ckmeadows
...meadows

Ramshaw Rocks

This conspicuous uplift in the landscape lies to the west of the
Leek Road, some eight miles south of Buxton, and comes as a
pleasant surprise after the bleak moors of Axe Edge. Seen on
the skyline long before they are reached, these strange
gritstone pinnacles and boulders are worthy of close
inspection and require only a few minutes to walk up to them
across the intervening moor. The most prominent crag
overhangs slightly and is shaped like a giant toad when
viewed from the ridge further to the south. The panorama
round the western arc is interesting and includes a back view
of Hen Cloud and the long crest of the Roaches.

Route 23. Drive along Axe Edge from Buxton and park your
car on the grass verge near the southern terminus of the ridge.
Attain the first of the prominent rocks and while walking
north examine each obelisk in turn and scramble to the top of
those that appeal to you.

Plate 24 R . . . M . . . Bradgate Park south

Plate 95 **Route 23**—Ramshaw Rocks—south

Hen Cloud

This shapely eminence stands to the north-west of the charming hamlet of Upper Hulme, which lies to the west of the A53 about a mile to the south of Ramshaw Rocks. It rises steeply from the moor and is crowned by a ring of symmetrical buttresses which, combined with its pyramidal form imparts to the whole the semblance of a real mountain.

While some of the crags afford exciting scrambling, there are at least three climbs that have long attracted the rock climber; they are Central Route, the Arete and the Great Chimney. There are more than 100 rock climbs on Hen Cloud alone. At fine weekends it is not unusual to encounter many of these sportsmen enjoying themselves high above the surrounding country.

Route 24. Follow Route 23 and continue your drive downhill in the direction of Leek, keeping a sharp look out for the signposted turn on the R to Upper Hulme. The road is narrow and at first descends steeply to a bridge, whence it passes through a mill yard and then turns sharp R uphill when Hen Cloud soon makes its appearance on the R. Park your car on the grass verge, pass through the scanty trees and then walk across the moor to the base of the hill. Make your way to its crest and wander along the skyline from buttress to buttress, then descend to the path below the crags and follow them to the end on the way back to your car.

Bow Buttress

Arete Climb

Route 96 **Route 24**—Climbers on Hen Cloud

Plate 97 **Route 21.** Hen Cloud from the south

Plate 98 **Route 24** — Finishing the climb Bow Buttress on Hen Cloud

The Roaches

These prominent bastions form the most imposing outcrop of
gritstone in the Pennines and vie in popularity with Stanage
Edge to which they draw the toughest rock climbers in the
country. The ridge crowned by these formidable buttresses
and slabs takes root half a mile to the north-west of Hen
Cloud and peters out at Roach End, two miles to the north.
When seen from the south they make an attractive picture,
with the afternoon sunlight catching the long line of crags
above a dark band of trees, but from other directions they are
by no means as conspicuous. Since these rocks flank a ridge
which falls steeply on the other side, they receive a greater
buffetting from wind and rain than the other outcrops so far
described. On this account they are subject to a greater degree
of erosion, a condition that is soon apparent to the climber.
They may be reached easily from the narrow lane which
continues from Hen Cloud, skirts the trees and goes on to
Roach End. But parking places are few and it is usually
advisable to run the car on to the grass verge nearby and leave
it there.

The Roaches are divided into two distinct bands of rock.
First there is the steep line of the Lower Tier, into whose base
has been built the Gamekeeper's cottage, embowered in trees.
To the L of it stone steps lead up to the more level ground
flanking the Upper Tier, in which the titanic slab of the Sloth,
with its gigantic overhang, is the most fantastic feature. Paths
meander in and out of the boulders and trees on this extensive
Promenade, from which the routes festooning the slabs,
chimneys, cracks and walls rise to a forbidding skyline. In this
particular section some of the climbs exceed 100 feet in height;
and of them all Saul's Crack and the Sloth used to be
considered the most difficult, until a new generation did many
much harder things, including the roof left of the Sloth.

At the terminal point of this Promenade there is a wide
break in the crags, and a path goes up a gully on the R beside
a wire fence. Beyond it, and level with the Upper Tier, the

rocks continue but are lower and more shattered. Skyline Buttress dominates this section and the adjacent crags form an admirable training ground for the beginner. There is a charming pool on the broad grassy ridge behind Skyline Buttress, whence a well worn track continues to Roach End. These rocks dominate a 100 acre Estate which was purchased in 1980 by the Peak Board. It is managed primarily as a nature reserve with access to climbers and walkers.

Route 25. Follow Route 24 to Hen Cloud and continue your drive to the point where the road sweeps round to the R. Stop here for a moment to admire the splendour of the Roaches ahead and then proceed to below the band of trees where you should park your car. Keep to one or other of the well trodden paths which lead to the keeper's cottage. Then walk up to examine the crags of the Lower Tier and climb on their L to the promenade which unfolds a comprehensive view of the first section of the rocks forming the Upper Tier.

Now walk to the L through the trees and scattered boulders below the long line of cliffs, and glance upwards from time to time to view their contorted elevation and overhangs. On reaching the break in the outcrop turn R up the gully and then L on the ridge and saunter along its lofty crest until you come to Roach End, meanwhile glancing round to scan the vast panorama. Then retrace your steps, but instead of descending the gully keep to the ridge and examine the strange rocks that crown it. If you are an experienced climber you may choose to descend one or other of the narrow breaks in the cliffs, but otherwise it is better to continue to the end of the ridge where a path will lead you downhill safely to your car.

It was through the kindness of Mr K. Meldrum that I was able to meet Mr Joe Brown and his pupil Mr John Amatt at the Roaches, and I wish to place on record my appreciation for their ready co-operation which enabled me to secure these photographs of their ascents of Saul's Crack and the Sloth.

Plate 99 The first view of the Roaches

Plate 100 **Route 25**—Joe Brown leads Saul's Crack

Plate 101 **Route 25**—Upper section of Saul's Crack

Overhang

The Pedestal

The Great Slab

Plate 102 **Route 25**—The Sloth

Plate 103 **Route 25**—John Amatt on the Pedestal

Plate 104 **Route 25**—Joe Brown leads the Overhang

Plate 105 **Route 25**—The crucial move

Plate 106 **Route 25**—Swing high!

The Castleton Caves

Castleton is pleasantly situated at the head of Hope Dale, a broad and pastoral valley which unhappily bears the scars of its industrial exploitation. The quaint houses of the village stand in the very shadow of Peveril Castle, which is a prominent object in the view of the dale and easily attained by a zig-zag path on the north side. It is, however, unassailable from all others, and its walls actually stand on the edge of the great gash in the hillside which encloses the entrance to the Peak Cavern, while on the south it overlooks the narrow ravine of Cave Dale.

The Peak Cavern is near the village and the approach to it discloses an impressive piece of rock architecture. Limestone cliffs, 300 feet high, tower overhead and trees cling to crannies in its sheer face where centuries ago a waterfall probably descended into the bed of the present river which issues from the cavern. The spectacular entrance is 114 feet wide, 40 feet high and of semicircular shape. For 400 years men and women made ropes and twine in this 300 feet long cavity where massive stalactites overhead assume the peculiar form of birds, animals and human figures. The passages shown to the public are half a mile in length and electrically illuminated throughout. The most striking features are the vast chambers, lofty *avens* and the Eight Arches which are found in the farthest recesses of the cavern. All these bear ample evidence of the tremendous force and mechanical action of the water and although the River Styx appears here and there in the passages in dry weather, they are soon flooded by heavy rains. Mr John Walker kindly conducted me through the Peak Cavern and pointed out its most arresting conformations. Ultimately it links, via an arduous caving expedition, with Speedwell.

The Speedwell Mine is situated at the foot of the Winnats and its famous cavern is reached by a straight subterranean canal

515 yards long. This was originally an eighteenth century lead mine whose promoters spent £14,000 and eleven years' ceaseless labour in tunnelling Long Cliff, only ultimately to abandon the whole project. At this distance from the entrance they encountered the Bottomless Pit and had to bridge it with a railed concrete platform before continuing the enterprise. They then tunnelled southwards for a further half mile to the Great Cliff Cavern with its two waterfalls about eighty feet high; but this extension of the canal is not shown to visitors. In the course of these excavations the miners flung 40,000 tons of debris into the Bottomless Pit whose dimensions were not ascertained until they were explored by J. W. Puttrell. He discovered the actual bottom to be ninety three feet from the platform and then by means of a raft secured the measurements of the underground lake at 1,900 square feet and 22 feet depth. The upper part of the cavern was explored in 1921 when the roof was found to be 140 feet above the platform, thus determining the total vertical height as 233 feet. The waters of this mysterious cavern reach the light of day at the Russet Well in Castleton. Mr H. Harrison gave me every facility and his son acted as my guide.

The Treak Cliff Caves are reached by a zig-zag path from the main road about a mile west of Castleton and are situated in the hillside to the north of the Winnats. They are electrically illuminated and famous for their stalactites, and also as the source of Blue John Stone for the last 150 years. Treak Cleft and the Blue John Caverns are the only places in the world where this stone is found and it has for years been worked into vases and other objects of art which grace many famous homes, the Vatican and even Pompeii. It was in the course of mining operations for Blue John in 1926 that the stalactite caves were discovered. There is a splendid array of these pendulous deposits of lime and their accepted rate of growth is one-sixteenth inch in a hundred years. This is a particularly fine example here which is thirty-six inches long and roughly estimated to be 36,000 years old. It will be another 1,000 years before it joins the shorter stalagmite rising to meet it. Mr John Royse was kind enough to conduct me through these caves.

The Blue John Caverns are entered under a rocky declivity facing the shattered front of Mam Tor and their inspection involves the descent of some 160 steps. A winding and undulating passage connects them and finally leads to a spacious chamber known as Lord Mulgrave's Dining Room which is thirty feet wide and 150 feet high. However, the most remarkable of these caverns is that known as the 'Waterfall' which is eighty feet high and one mass of stalagmites from floor to ceiling; the unique feature being the horizontal ribbing of the lime deposits side by side with the usual vertical forms. The latter are easily accounted for by the natural fall of the water, but so far no satisfactory explanation has been found for the appearance of the former which display a variety of colours ranging from pure white to jet black. Mr A. Ollerenshaw kindly showed me through these caverns and pointed out their many interesting features.

Route 26. Drive to Castleton and leave your car in the large park outside the Peak Cavern. After viewing it, drive on to the Speedwell Mine where you will have to descend 104 steps to the boat which is propelled by pushing at the roof of the canal with hands. In the eerie silence you glide forward until the first sounds of rushing water herald the approach of the Bottomless Pit. Step out on to the platform to observe the amazingly contorted rocks of both roof and pit. On returning to the surface drive back to the main road and turn sharp L for the Treak Cliff Caves. Park your car below the entrance and in due course observe with wonder the thirty-six inch stalactite which is the show piece of the cavern. Finally drive carefully up the Winnats Pass and park your car opposite Mam Tor on the R, then walk down to the Blue John Cavern entrance and take care while descending the 160 steps. And if you happen to be either a geologist or a speleologist the 'Waterfall' will prove of special interest.

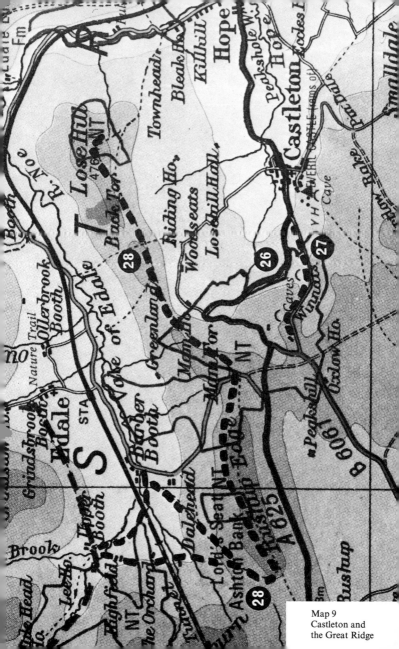

Map 9
Castleton and
the Great Ridge

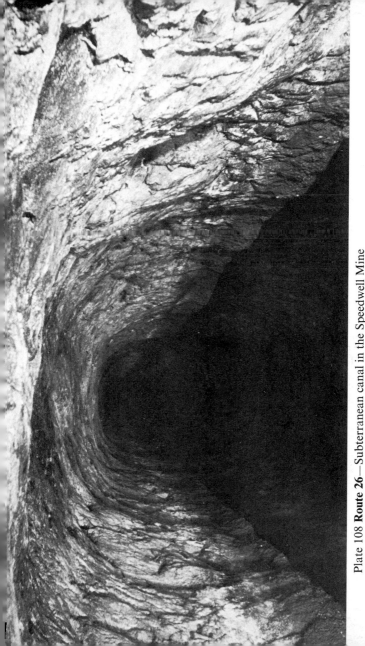

Plate 108 **Route 26**—Subterranean canal in the Speedwell Mine

Plate 110 **Route 26**—Waterfall Cavern—Blue John Mine

The Winnats

This is a narrow, sweeping pinnacled ravine which was originally formed by the action of water on the soft limestone of the district. In the course of centuries this produced a gigantic cavern which ultimately collapsed on the subsidence of the water. A steep road threads its entire length and has been used for testing motor cars. Its wide mouth begins almost opposite Speedwell Cavern and it narrows as height is gained to terminate in about a mile near Oxlow House.

Route 27. It is best to walk up the Winnats rather than down and is used by many pedestrians as the most interesting approach to Mam Tor and the Great Ridge from Castleton. But those with a steady head who desire to appreciate fully the splendour of this amazing gash in the landscape should walk up to the top and then turn L and walk back along the crest of the cliffs. Their dynamic elevation will then be more apparent, with the road far below and Win Hill in the far distance.

Plate 111 **Route 27** — The Winnats. Access is no longer restricted to those going to premises within, as the main Mam Tor road has collapsed

Win Hill

Plate 112 Photo 27. Win Hill from the crest of the Winnats

The Great Ridge

Rushup Edge	1,802 feet	550 metres
Mam Tor	1,695 feet	517 metres

This title calls for some comment and an explanation. I have used it primarily for convenience and to avoid repeating the names of its principal tops throughout this monograph. It is, however, more commonly known as the Mam Tor—Lose Hill Ridge and constitutes the great barrier which rises between Castleton and Edale.

The Great Ridge is the only one of its kind in the Peak District and in no section is it narrow enough to assume spectacular proportions. It is some four miles in length and a stone wall which runs along its crest is much damaged in several places. It may be ascended at almost any point and, in fact, many paths rise to the wall from both sides. It is a matter of opinion which direction makes the most enjoyable traverse, but after having walked both ways along it on several occasions I think photographers should go from west to east in the afternoon when the lighting is most advantageous. Mam Tor is its most striking feature and its shattered southern front looks its best from the neighbourhood of Castleton. A close view from its western edge is not only impressive, but also reveals the ridge trailing away to the east in which Back Tor is prominent.

Route 28. Whether you stay in Castleton or Edale matters little, but if you decide to leave your car behind and walk all the way you can ascend one end of the ridge and descend from the other. Otherwise, if you drive up to Mam Nick and park your car in the vicinity, you will have to walk to Lose Hill and back, unless someone drives the vehicle back to your lodgings.

Rushup Edge crowns the western extremity of the Great Ridge and if coming from Castleton you should walk up to it by way of the Winnats. But if you start from Edale you will have a choice of two routes. One of them leaves the road beyond the bridge over the River Noe at Barber Booth and goes by Chapel Gate, while the other leaves Upper Booth and merges with it before reaching the grassy summit near Lord's Seat. Halt here awhile near the cairn and scan the adjacent countryside, noting the tremendous whaleback which swings round to the north to join the Kinder plateau, the lengthy prospect of your ridge and the extensive vistas of the dales on either side. Then follow the broad path to the east along its crest where the approach to Mam Tor is quite dramatic, for the ridge in the vicinity narrows considerably although the drop on either side is neither tremendous nor precipitous.

Cross Mam Nick and ascend the path by the wall to Mam Tor, noting the remains of the prehistoric earthworks which are clearly visible. Then descend on the R as far as the rim of its shattered southern front which is almost sheer and due to the frosty disintegration of the alternate strata of hard gritstone and friable shale; this accounts for its popular name of the 'Shivering Mountain.' Return to the path on the Tor and continue your walk eastwards, and when you reach the col where the Edale-Castleton path crosses the ridge at Hollin's Cross observe the views of the valleys on either side. To the north, the village of Edale nestles at the entrance to Grindsbrook, while to the south many of the features of Hope Dale are disclosed in which Castleton, Peveril Castle and the Peak Cavern entrance are conspicuous.

As you walk along by the wall towards Back Tor you will probably agree that this is the most striking section of the traverse, for its crumbling precipices contrast well with the smooth green slopes of the ridge and the flat sky-line of the distant Edges. Follow the path skirting the Tor past the onetime plantation of pines of which only a few gnarled trees remain, and then wander up the gentle slope to Lose Hill whose shapely lines make a pleasant terminus to the ridge. Win Hill

has been conspicuous for some time and it is here seen to
dominate the long ridge on the opposite side of the valley. The
retrospect of the Great Ridge reveals its many ups and downs,
together with the massive elevation of Mam Tor and Rushup
Edge which block the western skyline.

Back Tor | Lose Hill

Plate 114 **Route 28**— The ridge from the cliffs of Mam Tor

Plate 115 **Route 29** Edale and Grindsbrook from the ridge

Plate 116 **Route 28**— Back Tor, now bereft of its plantation

Mam Tor — Rush up Edge

Plate 118 Edale Church and Grindsbrook

Kinder Scout

Kinder High	2,088 feet	636 metres
Crowden Head	2,064 feet	629 metres
Fairbrook Naze	2,049 feet	625 metres
Mill Hill	1,761 feet	537 metres

The Vale of Edale is so well situated for access to Kinder and
the many wild cloughs which deeply rift this great massif that
some notes on it may be welcome. It stretches for six miles in
a westerly direction from Edale End at the foot of Jagger's
Clough, two miles from Hope, to Jacob's Ladder in the very
shadow of Edale Head. It is bounded on the north by the
indented flanks of the High Peak and on the south by the
smoother and less lofty slopes of the Great Ridge. The
entrance to the dale is comparatively narrow and lies at the
north-eastern foot of Lose Hill. It widens considerably as it
extends westwards, but beyond Barber Booth bends in a
north-westerly direction and after passing Upper Booth at the
foot of Crowden Brook, ends in the recesses of Kinder just
beyond Jacob's Ladder.

Both road and rail pass through the valley; the former
turns to the south at Barber Booth and after climbing steeply
and sinuously, it passes through the narrow gap of Mam Nick
to join the Castleton-Chapel highway on the southern flanks
of Rushup Edge; the latter gives direct access to the dale from
Manchester and Sheffield and is much patronised by hikers
from these great cities as is evidenced by the crowds arriving
at Edale Station at fine weekends.

Several charming hamlets grace the valley and their names
at once impart a romantic glamour to their surroundings; for
what could sound more attractive than Nether Booth or
Barber Booth? Edale is, of course, the principal village with its
Information Office and large car park but is more correctly
known as Grindsbrook Booth! Its beautiful church stands on
the 800 feet contour at the entrance to this cavernous recess

which penetrates deeply into the Peak and is frowned upon by Grindslow Knoll and Ringing Roger, two lofty eminences rising on either side of the clough.

The Kinder Plateau covers a vast area and is about five miles long and three miles wide. It is intersected in all directions by slippery peat groughs which drain off the water in rainy weather, and scarcely rises anywhere above the 2,000 feet contour. It can justly be described as a sinister mountain and its extensive summit a notoriously dangerous place in bad weather. The most popular ascents from Edale are Crowden Brook and Grindsbrook and the circuit of its lofty Edges affords an invigorating tramp, but the highlight of the whole plateau is Kinder Downfall which is some 100 feet high. In calm dry weather it sports a trickle of water only, whereas after heavy rain, accompanied by a strong south-westerly wind which rushes through the gigantic natural funnel below it like a hurricane, the fall is blown back over its crest and provides one of the most astonishing spectacles in the country. However, striking as this scene may be in summer, it is incomparably more beautiful when observed under severe winter conditions; for it is then draped with gigantic icicles which hang from the ledges and scintillate in the afternoon sunlight.

It should be noted that most of the access points to Kinder are signposted and that grouse should not be disturbed during the nesting season from Mid-April to Mid-June. Moreover, notice boards are displayed in the area to inform walkers on which days between August 12th and December 10th the moors are closed to the public for grouse shooting.

The buttresses of Kinder Scout, together with the gritstone tors and outcrops which are widely distributed on the perimeter of the plateau, are less than 100 feet in height but afford an attractive playground for the rock climber. They are divided into three separate groups, as follows: 1. the Tors flanking the Fairbrook area on the northern Edges include Quadrinnacle, Cabin Buttress, Fairbrook Buttress, Pavlova and Chinese Wall; 2. the Outcrops adjacent to Grindsbrook

Map 10
Kinder Scout

Alport
Alport Dale
Alport Castles
NT
Birchinlee Pasture
Swint Clough
Ouzelden Clough
Cowms Rocks
Rowlee Pasture
Hey Ridge
(course of)
Upper Ho.
Wood Hos
Ashop
A 57
NT
E
Woodlands Valley
Hagg Fm
30
31
Edge
Crookstone Knoll
Blackden Brook
Ashop Moor
Jaggers Clough
30
Nether Moor
Oller Brook
YH
Nether Booth
31
Carr Ho.
Edale Fm
Ollerbrook Booth
R. Noe
Lose Hill
476m
NT
Back Tor
Vale of Edale

above Edale including Ringing Roger, Nether Tor, Upper Tor and Grindsbrook Rocks and Towers; 3. the Cliffs enclosing Kinder Downfall include the Great Buttress, the Amphitheatre, Kinder Buttress and the Upper and Lower Western Buttresses. Group 1 is the most distant and only reached conveniently from the Snake Inn or by a long tramp from Hayfield. The Great Buttress is perhaps the best known as it yields a remarkable sense of exposure owing to the steepness of the ground which sweeps down to the Kinder River far below. However, climbers should note that rock falls have occurred on Nether Tor where exceptional care is now vital.

Route 29. This is one of the classic ascents of the High Peak and the most direct approach to Kinder Downfall from Edale. It leaves the valley at Upper Booth, threads Crowden Brook and passes its conspicuous Tower perched on the edge of the plateau, crosses the wilderness of peat groughs to the Kinder River which is then followed to the Downfall. This Route may involve the use of a compass and should be severely left alone in bad weather.

Take the field path from Edale to Upper Booth but leave it for the higher track at the entrance to the clough. It passes above a pine wood and then unfolds a grand prospect of Crowden Brook in its entirety. Join the track by the stream which descends over a maze of boulders to form attractive cascades and climb up beside it. On reaching the waterfall below the skyline, keep to the L and then proceed to Crowden Tower. This is a splendid viewpoint for the appraisal of the dreary and almost level wilderness of peat groughs which stretch as far as the eye can see. Now follow the R branch of the brook almost to Crowden Head, whence bear slightly west of north to pick up the Kinder River. Follow its sandy bed to the immense boulders blocking the top of the Downfall and note Hayfield Reservoir glittering in the sunlight far below. Finally walk round the rim of its enclosing walls and observe the gymnastics of any climbers who happen to be there.

Crowden Tower

Plate 119 **Route 29**—Crowden Brook

Plate 120 Route 20. The Kinder Plateau from Crowden Tower

Plate 121 **Route 29**—The Kinder River

Plate 122 **Route 29**— Havfield Reservoir from the Downfall

Plate 123 **Route 29**—Kinder Downfall in summer

Route 30. The most interesting expedition from Edale is the circuit of the Kinder Edges which are famous for the strange obelisks of gritstone that are encountered during a walk of some fifteen miles. The only strenuous section is the direct ascent of the 1,000 feet from the village to Ringing Roger, whose prominent collection of boulders and stones lie on the lip of the plateau.

Leave Edale by the Pennine Way and on entering the wide mouth of Grindsbrook bear R up the grassy slopes of the High Peak. On attaining Ringing Roger note the fine vista of this clough on the L, and then walk eastwards with views on the R of Jagger's Clough. Now cross the end of the plateau by bearing L to reach Blackden Edge which commands a splendid prospect of the Snake, backed by Bleaklow. Thence walk in a westerly direction along the well worn path, past the outcrop of Seal Edge which opens up the first view of Fairbrook Naze, high above Ashop Clough. Continue along the northern rim of the plateau, cross the shelf-like course of Fair Brook and then ascend the shattered flanks of the Naze which is admirably situated for lunch. After this welcome rest proceed along the lofty crest of Ashop Edge and note the strange obelisks which stand on its rim, and particularly those known as the 'Boxing Gloves' which are a famous landmark. Observe also the whole course of Ashop Clough spread out below and backed by the barren moors of Featherbed Moss. When you reach the spur overlooking William Clough, turn L to the south-east for Kinder Downfall whose grim bastions frown upon the little Mermaid's Pool far below. Continue your walk southwards past Red Brook and make for the cairn on Kinder Low which unfolds nothing more interesting than a spectacle of utter desolation. If desired you may proceed in a southerly direction to Edale Cross and descend to the valley by Jacob's Ladder, but it is more interesting to follow the rim of the Plateau eastwards to Pym's Chair and eventually to the Anvil which is poised on the very edge of Grindsbrook. Finally complete your long tramp by descending the Pennine Way to Edale and your well-earned supper.

Plate 124 **Route 30**—Grindsbrook from Ringing Roger

Plate 125 Route 30. Fairbrook Naze from Seal Edge

Plate 126 **Route 30**—Strange Rocks on Ashop Edge

Plate 127 Route 29. The Boxing Glove Stones

Plate 128 **Route 30**—Pym's Chair

Plate 129 **Route 30**—The Anvil overlooks Grindsbrook

Route 31. The circuit of the Kinder itself is an expedition of first importance and its twenty-two miles of varied scenery will appeal to strong walkers who may complete it in a day, but can, if desired, finish their ambulations at Hayfield and return to Edale by bus and train from Chinley Junction. The walk may be undertaken in either direction, but those who wish to see the vast amphitheatre enclosing Kinder Downfall by afternoon or evening light should go from east to west in the section from the Snake Inn.

Leave Edale by the pack-horse bridge and cross the field to join the road at Nether Booth. A short step beyond this hamlet you take the path on the L, mount the hillside and then drop down to cross the sparkling stream in Jagger's Clough. Now take the L branch at the fork in the path and continue to the Woodlands Valley where Alport Dale and its Castles appear ahead. Cross the footbridge over the Alport River and on reaching the road turn L for the Snake Inn, noting on the L the magnificent prospect of Seal Edge and Fairbrook Naze on the lofty skyline. On a hot summer day you will doubtless linger here to take refreshment and then, after walking a few yards up the road, turn L over a stile in a gap in the trees to cross the stream and enter the wild valley of Ashop Clough.

Keep to the path on the L bank of the stream all the way to its source at Ashop Head, meanwhile observing the great barrier on the other side of it crowned by Ashop Edge. On and on you go until the track peters out in a sea of mud where stakes driven into the ground will guide you in safety to the col leading over to William Clough. Here the scene changes dramatically, for instead of descending through a barren wilderness you drop downhill by a trickling stream which threads a ravine clothed in heather, bracken, ferns and trees. Hayfield Reservoir now appears below and you skirt its west side to pick up the track for Edale. Pause here for a few moments to admire the magnificent prospect on your L which reveals to perfection the gigantic amphitheatre enclosing the Downfall. Now climb the spur ahead which skirts the Kinder bluffs and leads to Edale Cross, whence continue along the path and descend Jacob's Ladder for Barber Booth and Edale.

During 1982 the National Trust acquired for a sum in the region of £600,000, more than 3000 acres of the Hayfield Estate, which includes the moorland plateau of Kinder Scout, Kinder Downfall, part of Edale Moor and two farms with their resident flock of sheep.

Bleaklow and Doctor's Gate

Bleaklow Head	2,060 feet	628 metres
Higher Shelf Stones	2.039 feet	622 metres
The Snake	1,680 feet	512 metres

Bleaklow is the vast, rifted moorland uplift to the north of Kinder and separated from it by the A57 which crosses the Snake between Ladybower and Glossop. The characteristic difference between the two is that whereas the latter is crowned by a nearly level plateau whose flanks are steep, the former displays massive sloping shoulders whose area above the 1,750 feet contour is about the same but considerably less above 2,000 feet. This wilderness of grass, bog and peat grough is dominated by the flat, broad ridge of Bleaklow Hill which is nearly two miles in length and terminates in the east at Bleaklow Stones and in the west at Bleaklow Head. With the exception of these two points, and possibly also Higher Shelf Stones located near the latter which can often be picked out from the southern arc of the moor, the whole area is lacking in landmarks. In consequence those who venture away from the well marked paths through Doctor's Gate or the Pennine Way should have company and always carry both map and compass. This sinister mountain should never be explored by the lone climber, even in clear weather, and his only safe wandering should always be in sight of the traffic passing over the Snake.

Bleaklow is riven on every side by cloughs whose streams drain off the water from the higher ground, and the longest of them all is the Alport River. Its tributaries have their source on the south side of Bleaklow Hill and their water is received eventually by Ladybower Reservoir in the Woodlands Valley. Alport Dale is well known for its conspicuous Castles which may be attained from the A57.

Some conception of the utter wildness of the massif may be

obtained by walking through Doctor's Gate, where the well trodden track is some three miles in length. It begins at the sharp bend on the A57 below Shire Hill, just over a mile from Glossop, and goes to Mossylee where the Shelf Brook is crossed by a footbridge. Thence it rises at an easy gradient beside the stream and in its higher reaches is flanked on the north by Shelf Moor, dominated by Higher Shelf Stones, which is the most impressive section of the walk.

After passing Gathering Hill and Crooked Clough on the L, it follows the stones which are remnants of the old Roman Road and descends ultimately to the main highway to join it at Doctor's Gate Culvert. The Pennine Way crosses this path in sight of Crooked Clough, and its muddy track traverses the edge of Devil's Dike, swings round to the L at the foot of Hern Clough, and thence goes due north to Bleaklow Head.

Gritstone outcrops on Bleaklow are surprisingly few and far between, and the only one of note on its western flanks is Yellow Slacks (damaged by explosions in July 1963 and February 1964) above the Brook of the same name, and reached easily from Mossylee. However, there are two outcrops on its northern slopes, Shining Clough and Torside Clough, both of which may be attained from Crowden in the Longdendale Valley.

Route 32. Any motorist who is a strong walker may leave his car in the bay on the north side of the road at Doctor's Gate Culvert, traverse the more interesting upper section of Doctor's Gate and then go on to Bleaklow Head on a fine and clear summer day.

If you are staying at the Snake Inn, drive up the busy highway through Lady Clough and park your car near the notice board at the Culvert, which is about half a mile short of the summit of the Snake. But should you come from Glossop you will drive up the A57 through Holden Clough, pass the summit and drive downhill to park your car in the same place near the bridge. Take your map and compass which will be indispensable if the weather deteriorates, and set off up the winding path which rises to the stony section of the old Roman Road. Then go downhill until the glittering Shelf Brook appears ahead and follow the path on its L as far as the point where it emerges on to more open ground. Now retrace your steps and note the fine elevation of the Higher Shelf Stones, now on your L, and on attaining the higher rim of Crooked Clough pick up the Pennine Way. This goes sharp L along Devil's Dike and is a well marked peat track all the way to Bleaklow Head; doubtless due to the thousands of walkers on the Pennine Way. During a dry spell the path is easily negotiable whereas after heavy rain it becomes a sticky quagmire.

If you omit the approach from Doctor's Gate Culvert you will start from the summit of the Snake, whence for about a quarter of a mile a plastic paraweb footpath had been laid some years ago over one of the wettest sections of this route. However, more recently this was removed as unsatisfactory, and has now been replaced by a combination of forestry brashings, chestnut pile fencing and other materials. Thence a series of prominent stakes mark your way and can be well seen in clear weather. They were erected voluntarily in 1966 by pupils of Chesterfield Grammar School to mark the boundary between the parishes of Charlesworth and Hope Woodlands. After passing Alport Low the track goes through the lower section of Hern Clough where a stream snakes from side to side while the track keeps straight on. You will probably commence by jumping the stream, but it gets so tiring that you will eventually walk straight through, hoping your boots will have been adequately waterproofed! At the end of this wet section the Wain Stones appear on the distant skyline, a welcome landmark on this desolate moorland. On attaining them, Bleaklow Head appears against the sky on the flat top of the moor and you have attained your objective.

It should be noted that these moors are closed to the public on certain days for grouse shooting and details are specified on boards at the Snake and Doctor's Gate Culvert.

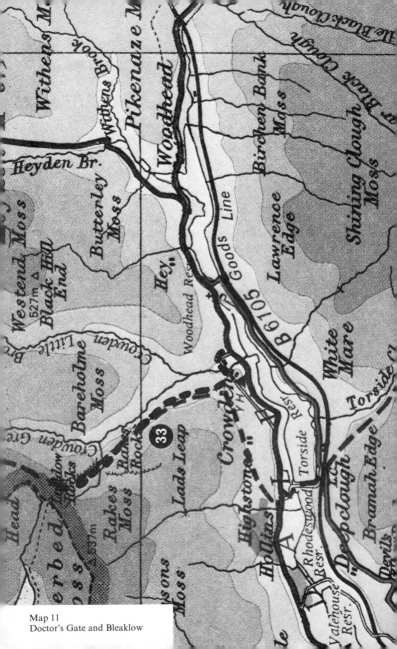

Map 11
Doctor's Gate and Bleaklow

Cock Hill
Moss
Swineshaw Resr.
Small Clough
Dowstone Clough
Shelf Moss
P
32
Hosp.
Moorside
Old Glossop
Higher Shelf Stones
Shire Hill
Shelf Moor
Mossylee
Hern Clough
Shelf Brook
A57
Hurst
GLOSSOP
Devils
Alport
32
Carr
9
Hurst Resr.
Whitfield Ho.
Hurstnook
Coldharbour Moor
Jumble
NT
Gate
Grindlesg
Span Moor
Span Clough
Hurst Moor
Moorfield
Bray Clough
Featherbed Top
Black Moor
Moss Castle
Featherbed Moss
Lady Clough

Plate 120 Route 22. The beginning of the Roman road

Plate 131 **Route 32**— Remains of the Roman road

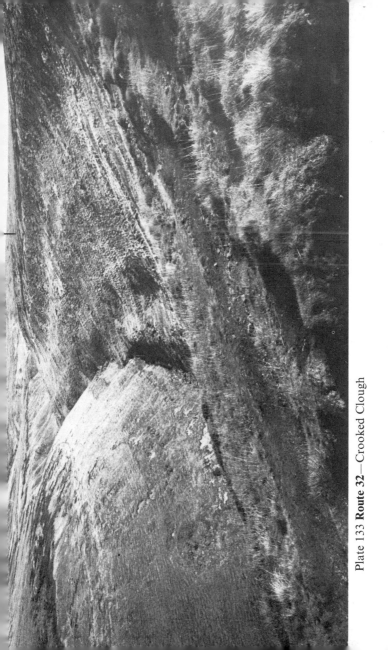

Plate 133 **Route 32**—Crooked Clough

Plate 124 Route 22. The summit of the Snake, the track to Blacklow Head starts here

Plate 135 **Route 32**—Higher Shelf Stones from the junction with Doctor's Gate

PLATE 106. Bank's Moss Pass; a track has made the direction of the Pennine Way

Plate 137 **Route 32** — Walkers on the Pennine Way. Devil's Dyke on the left

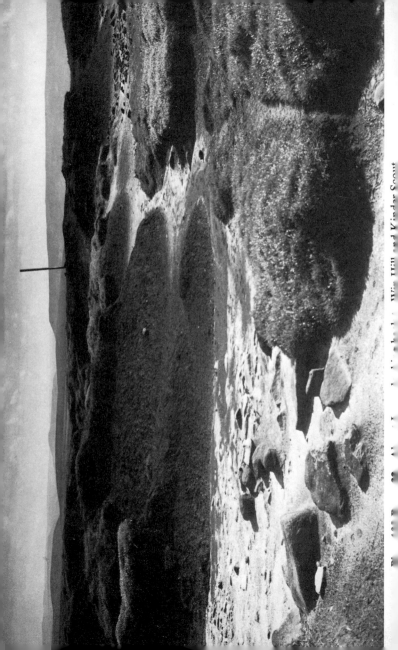

Win Hill and Kinder Scout

Plate 139 **Route 32** — The head of Hern Clough

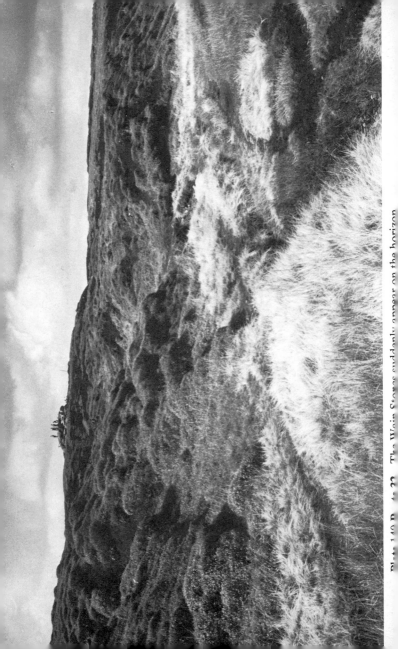

Plate 149 B to 22. The Wain Stones suddenly appear on the horizon

Plate 141 **Route 32**— Wain Stones, the first prominent landmark

Bleaklow Head

Plate 123B. Bleaklow Head from the Snake at Wain Stones

Laddow

These rocks are the most northerly and at the same time the most isolated of the important gritstone outcrops in the Peak District National Park. They flank the very edge of the lofty moor, high up on the west of Crowden Great Brook and are just over two miles from Crowden on the busy A628. As one of the most famous, and possibly also one of the earliest playgrounds of the rock climber, these fine Towers have since attracted legions of mountaineers owing to their height and steepness, together with their commanding situation over the valley which conveys a sense of exposure akin to that of the Great Buttress on Kinder Scout.

There are two approaches to Laddow: the shorter and more popular starts at Crowden where there is parking space for several cars in a narrow side road, and on which route the cliffs are often visible on the skyline ahead; the longer and less used starts at Greenfield and takes a southeasterly course up Chew Valley, passes Chew Reservoir and then goes over the moor to the top of the rocks which are invisible until they are reached. Pedestrians without transport may prefer to approach them by the latter and return by the former; the time taken for this walk is about three hours which makes no allowance for climbing, and the whole route opens up a continuous array of wild scenery.

The cliffs extend for only about 200 yards, and it is inadvisable to leave the Crowden track before they are reached, despite the fact that a direct approach seems shorter. It is better to follow the path along the crest to the end of the outcrop and descend a steep rake which goes down on the R to a cave, a welcome retreat in bad weather. The track turns R round the base of the first buttress and undulates below the towers and chimneys. Considering the long use of Laddow as a climbers' playground, the crags are unexpectedly dirty as in heavy rain sand is washed down the face of the cliffs and fills the holds. The principal routes from L to R are Priscilla Ridge, Slab and Long Climb, Long Chimney, Straight

Chimney, Tower Face, North Wall and Cave Crack.

Route 33. If you are a climber and a motorist, you will not hesitate to choose Crowden as the starting point for Laddow and will drive to the conspicuous cottages and Youth Hostel on the north side of the A628. Continue along the lane which swings round to the L and ends near a bridge where further progress is barred by a gate across the road. Here you will have only enough space to turn a small car, but if it is a large one it is easier to reverse into a side lane nearby and leave it on the grass verge.

Go through the gate and walk uphill along a cart track until a fingerpost indicates your route to the R. Follow the wire fence for some distance and then keep to the track which rises at an easy gradient along the hillside above Crowden Great Brook. Cross a footbridge that is romantically placed in sight of Rakes Rocks and then ascend the little hill ahead whose summit reveals clearly for the first time your objective on the distant skyline. Do not leave the path until it attains the edge of the moor and then bear to the R until you reach the far end of the crags. Now scramble down the steep rake and follow the track below the towers and chimneys, and if it happens to be raining take shelter in the cave at the foot of the rake.

This is my last subject in the delectable countryside of the Peak District National Park, and I shall now cross the industrial belt farther north to reach the Yorkshire Pennines. Here the crags on Ilkley Moor will receive due notice and thereafter the important outcrops, potholes, hills and dales as far north as Hadrian's Wall.

Plate 143 **Route 33**—The first clear view of Laddow

The Scoop ————

Plate 144 **Route 33**—The Long Climb from above

Plate 145 **Route 33**—The Long Climb from below

Plate 146 **Route 33**—Tower Face from above

Twin Eliminate Tower Face

Tower Arete

North Wall

Plate 147 **Route 33**—Tower Face from below

Pulpit

Straight Chimney

Long Chimney

Anvil

Plate 148 **Route 33**—The Anvil Buttress

Ilkley

This well-known resort is spread along the banks of the River
Wharfe and frowned upon from the south by the brim of its
famous moor. As a lofty stretch of wild country, it is popular
with ramblers and opens up to the north extensive views of
the dale, backed by Blubberhouses Moor. But it is also a
favourite venue of the rock climber, since it exhibits three
separate groups of crags, of which two consist of eroded
gritstone and the third of sandstone—a quarry. All of them
flank the rim of the moor and are situated only about a mile
from the centre of the town. They are reached by the road
that eventually passes through Burley Woodhead and
Hawksworth to Guiseley, and on attaining the Cow and Calf
Hotel the most prominent of them is revealed on the R. This is
the renowned Cow and Calf, and some 200 yards to its L is
the Quarry, while half a mile to the south-west are the
buttresses of Rocky Valley.

The Cow is a well defined buttress about 60 feet high and
the Calf a gigantic boulder below it. There are many climbs on
these rocks. The Quarry nearby has two main walls, North and
South, which are opposite each other. The Eastern entrance is
between them at one end and enclosed at the other by a
shattered wall. Their height does not exceed about 60 feet.
Botterill's Crack is one of the classic ascents and is named after
this famous Yorkshire mountaineer, who pioneered many of
the routes on the British Hills which includes the notorious
Botterill's Slab on Scafell in English Lakeland.

The sandstone walls of the Quarry are an excellent training
ground with modern hard climbs like Wellington Crack. Plates
150 and 151 show instructors demonstrating the ascent of
Josephine which has a very delicate move below the exit.

Rocky Valley, known also as Ilkley Crags, may be seen on
the crest of the Moor when looking south-west from the top
of the Cow. The well worn path rising to its entrance crosses a
stream by some flat slabs, but on reaching it only five of the
six buttresses are revealed on the L. The most westerly No. 6 is

round a corner in the path and lower down than the others; it presents a fine rock face. Between Nos. 5 and 6 a steep track rises to the southern rim of the valley and continues eastwards past the top of each buttress. The large rock face of No. 1 Buttress is known as 'Cooper's Slab'.

Hawk Cliff Crag, consisting of firm gritstone and situated on private ground at Steeton, was explored by Brian Emmerson. It is about 350 yards in length and has more than 15 routes, the longest being the Central Buttress.

Route 34. Drive up to the moor and park your car on the R opposite the hotel. Walk up to the Cow and Calf and climb up to the top of the Cow for the fine panorama spread out below, then enter the Quarry to examine its sandstone walls and finally stroll to Rocky Valley.

Plate 149 **Route 34**— The Cow and Calf

Plate 150 **Route 34**—Quarry—N. wall. Ascent of Josephine

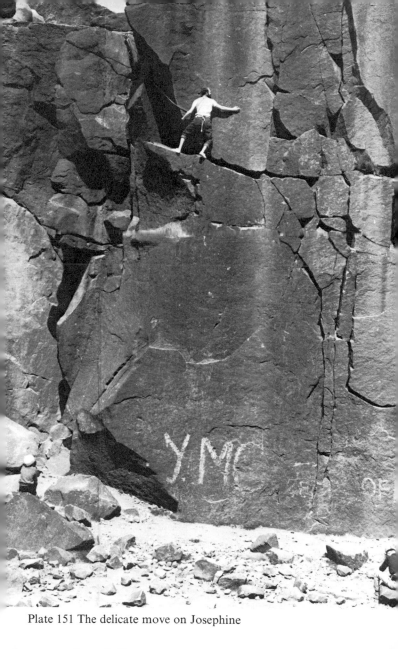

Plate 151 The delicate move on Josephine

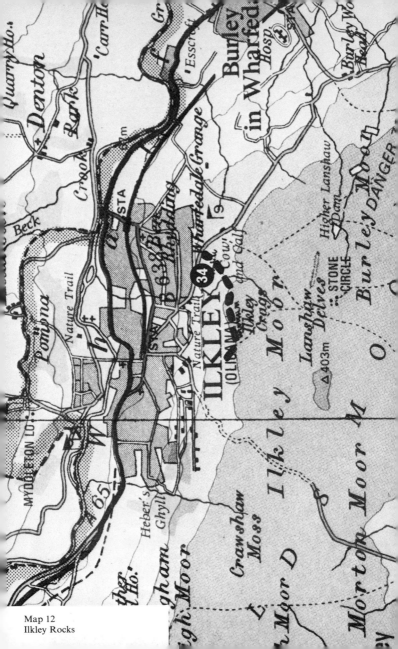

Map 12
Ilkley Rocks

Plate 152 Rocky Valley—the 5 buttresses

Plate 183 Rock Wall No. 6 buttress

Almscliff

This conspicuous gritstone outcrop crowns a small hill that rises about a mile due north of Huby, a village opposite Weeton Station and near the busy A658 between Pool and Harrogate. It is also less than a mile due west of Rigton, another village not far from this highway, but a narrow road connecting the two passes close to the south of the prominent crags which are usually approached from this side.

Almscliff is a relatively small outcrop and scarcely more than 100 yards in length, but it assumes a unique appearance owing to its division into two tiers, High and Low Man. The former might well be two adjacent Dartmoor Tors, separated by a narrow break called the Rift, which together form a semicircular façade that swings round from south to north. Level ground stretches some thirty yards to the crest of Low Man which merges with the hillside to the south, whereas to the north it terminates with a vertical buttress some forty feet high, below which lies the Matterhorn Boulder.

Festooned all along these faces are numerous courses, some of which were originated by the three famous mountaineers, Botterill, Frankland and Dolphin. Their hardest climbs are found on the most northerly front of High Man, and include Z Climb, and Central Climb and Frankland's Green Crack. None of them exceed a height of sixty feet. It is possible that the pioneering of this crag was done by Slingsby around 1865, and the first routes established about 1870. These are characterised by round holds, round cracks and round chimneys, and to successfully climb them involves an intimate knowledge of jamming—by hand, foot, arm, leg and body. Modern climbers have added many more even harder climbs, each generation leaving its legacy—like Wall of Horrors (Alan Austen, 1960s) and its successors.

Route 35. If you come from Harrogate turn R from the A658 for Rigton, then L, R and again L in the village, beyond which point Almscliff soon appears to the R of the road. Park your vehicle on the grass verge near a wall on the L where there is room for only about six small cars, then cross the road and pass over a stile whence a path leads up to the outcrop. But if you come from Pool, turn L for Huby and drive up the rising road until you are opposite the crag, then turn sharp R to reach the above mentioned parking place. Walk round the western front of each crag and then make the easy climb to the top from the east side which almost merges with the hill.

Map 13
Almscliff

Plate 155 **Route 35**— Low Man, with Matterhorn boulder on left

Plate 156 Route 25 High Man North with rift on the right

Plate 157 **Route 35**—High Man South

Plate 158 **Route 35**—Climbing Frankland's Green Crack

Brimham Rocks

This fantastic collection of gritstone rocks stands on the top of Brimham Moor and covers an area of some sixty acres. It is just over three miles due east of Pateley Bridge, under two miles north of Summer Bridge and seven miles south-west of Ripon. The least confusing approach is from Pateley Bridge by B6265 which attains its highest point at Crossgates, whence a signposted and walled lane goes off to the R. It skirts the Estate and then turns sharp R to a gate, with adjacent commodious car parks. Walkers proceed along the rough road which now winds in and out of the rocks, finally to reach a large open space beneath Brimham House which has recently been restored, and beside which a small building affords shelter in bad weather and also provides refreshments in the summer season. Brimham Rocks are now owned by the National Trust.

That these rocks are a geological freak will be apparent to all who wander round the Estate, and the grotesque shapes of the pinnacles, buttresses, leaning tors and boulders are ample evidence of the powerful eroding qualities of wind, water and frost. Rock Climbing began here over a century ago, but until the 1950's the area was rarely visited. From this date, however, the popularity of these rocks increased by leaps and bounds and it would be safe to say that there are few of our toughest rock climbers who have not worked out new routes on most of the obelisks. The rock is extremely rough and when climbed on wet days in winter the hands of the climber become scarred and cut by what is now known as 'gritstone rash'. The hardest climbs will be found along the Edge which lies to the west of the house and is perhaps 1,000 yards in length. Every mountaineer who happens to be in the vicinity should visit this fantastic rock garden, even if only to examine its fabulous collection and from time to time drowse in the prolific heather. A maze of paths gives access to every obelisk, but to see them all leisurely requires a whole day.

Similar formations will be found at PLUMPTON ROCKS on

A661, south-east of Harrogate. Most of them are hidden by the dense growth of trees, but the group overlooking the lake is clearly revealed. They are on a private estate, but can be inspected by the payment of a small fee.

Route 36. Those who stay as far away as Wharfedale, Ripon or Harrogate will have no difficulty in discovering Brimham Rocks if they follow the above directions, but they should choose a sunny day for the visit and if they are photographers will find the colours most brilliant and ravishing in the late autumn. After four visits and a detailed exploration of the whole Estate I have come to the conclusion that the best plan is to walk from the car park past the House and then to the rocks on the western perimeter of the area. A good starting point is the conspicuous Druid's Idol which is estimated to weigh 200 tons and is poised in perfect balance on a base measuring only twelve inches in diameter! Thence it is advisable to make a rough circle by north, east and south back to the starting point, from which route all the most curiously shaped rocks can be examined in detail.

36

Map 14
Brimham Rocks

Plate 159 **Route 36**—The Druid's Idol

Plate 160 **Route 36**—The Knob

Plate 161 **Route 36**—The Druid's Writing Desk

Plate 162 **Route 36**—Crown Rock and Kissing Chair

Plate 16. Rotorua. Kerosene Creek. Rocks

Plate 164 **Route 36**—The Dancing Bear

Plate 165 **Route 36**—The Turtle

Plate 166 **Route 36**—Plumpton Rocks

Stump Cross Caverns

The entrance to these caves is at an altitude of over 1,100 feet on the south side of B6265, a wild, windswept moorland road connecting Grassington with Pateley Bridge, and situated six miles from the former and five miles from the latter. The discovery of this underground system was due to an accidental breakthrough by a party of lead miners about 1860, and although unsuccessful in their venture they left behind a permanent way into the natural caverns. At the time of writing, the entrance was by way of an artificial stairway, of which the lower half is in a natural fissure where the first stalagtites can be seen suspended from the roof. Thence the path is clean and tidy, and the electric lighting throughout, sometimes coloured, is adequate for the close examination of each and every formation.

It was in Stump Cross Caverns that Mr Geoffrey Workman established his world record for a sojourn in complete solitude underground, with no outside contact other than a phone link, for 105 days from June 16th to September 29th, 1963. He spent his time by making a geological survey, and attempted by several digs to extend the lower cave, unfortunately without success.

I was received by the late Mr George Gill and Mrs Barbara Hanley who not only gave me every facility but provided welcome refreshment on a cold autumn day. I spent two hours underground with Mr Peter Charles, a well-known Birmingham pot-holer, who kindly guided me through the Caverns and also assisted me with their photography.

Route 37. Drive to the Caverns and leave your car in the spacious park behind the hut and near the entrance. Walk carefully down the steps and on turning to the L observe a door on the L which gives access to the lower series of caves in which Mr Workman established his world record. Passing the display of delicate straw stalactites on the R, you soon reach the Butcher's Shop which reveals a fine collection of both stalactites and stalagmites whose red and brown colouring is due to the presence of iron salts. The Twins and Jewel Box follow in quick succession, and then low down appears the Hawk. You will soon encounter the Sentinel, a column from floor to roof that is $9\frac{1}{2}$ feet in height and whose age is reputed to be well over 10,000 years. Next comes the Chamber of Pillars, illuminated by coloured fluorescent lighting, and then the remarkable Cradle which is actually a draped fallen boulder. Other attractive formations appear on either side of the passage until you reach the end of the cavern where a surprising display of reindeer Bones and the Wedding Cake will complete your interesting exploration.

Map 15
Lower Wharfedale

Craven 404m

B 6265 Dry Gill 37 Moor

Br. Stump Cross Caverns

Bancarl Ho.

Black Hill

ewick re

Tarn Gill

Trotter's Gill

PERCIVAL HALL

nd Ho.

Pock Stones

High Skyreholme

ls Middle Skyreholme

ick

Simon's Seat
485m △

Hen Stones

327

Howgill

Barden

Mark Brow

449m
Earl Seat

Fell

Brown Bank Head

Roo

△ 410m

Agill Ho.

Pocking Hall

Broad Shaw

Waterfall

Ho.

Waterfall

The Strid

Valley of Desolation

Hazlewood

Bolton Moor

Laund Ho.

Nature

Park

Wharfedale

This enchanting valley lies in the bosom of the Pennines, and its spacious curves stretch northwards from the very threshold of some of our great industrial cities to peter out in the distant fastnesses of the hills about Oughtershaw. The lower section as far as Threshfield and Grassington is richly wooded and flecked with historic buildings, whereas the trees thin out higher up, limestone crags appear, and beyond Kettlewell the hills close in until it merges finally with the desolate moors which separate it from Ribblesdale. The lower reaches of the dale are well seen on foot from Bolton Abbey, Burnsall or Grassington, while the more remote corners can be explored from Kettlewell or Buckden.

Although the rocks on Simon's Seat have received some attention from climbers, the only great problem in Wharfedale is Kilnsey Crag whose terrific limestone façade overhangs B6160 and is the eastern terminal point of the Craven Fault. For some years it had occupied the attention of members of the Rock and Ice Club, whose attempts on the Routes known as A, B and C had been unsuccessful. Then on March 24th, 1957 came success when Ron Moseley, Fred Williams, Barry Knox and J. A. Sumner completed the climb by first ascending Route B and then, by the use of five-sixteenth inch coach screws with fibre plugs and etriers, continued to the L under the roof of the main overhang and by a groove just beyond its greatest width reached the Brink and completed the ascent. But these tough members of the Rock and Ice Club had spent some time in preparation and in fact camped under the crag for five weekends getting a little farther across the roof on each visit. On the successful ascent Moseley was in etriers for eleven hours before he disappeared over the Brink to gain a small ledge on the vertical section of the roof. Mr Sumner tells me that the three coach screws on the Brink are still sound after twenty years. Despite the fact that this cliff is only 200 feet high, this dynamic ascent involved some 300 feet of sensational rock climbing, due to the above mentioned move to the L where the main overhang juts out some thirty-five feet from the vertical wall. This climb remains a legitimate aided ascent, but many very hard free climbs have now been pioneered on the buttresses nearby.

Route 38. Providing you have a car for the exploration of Wharfedale, and assuming you have already visited the crags on Ilkley Moor described in a previous monograph, it is advisable to begin your drive at Bolton Abbey. Park your car in the space provided on the L, and enter the grounds to see the famous Abbey, of which the transepts and choir are in ruins. Bolton Hall stands just behind it and the manor is held by the Dukes of Devonshire. Walk down to the river and cross the bridge, and if you are interested in the general view of the Abbey walk up the path to the tree-clad escarpment whose rocky base acts as a breakwater in the sharp curve of the wide stream. Return to your car and continue your drive up the dale, noting the Hole in the Wall on the R which is a well-known gap in the park enclosure. Continue for about two miles and park your car in the space provided on the R near the entrance to the Strid. Walk down to it through Bolton Woods and admire the water play, but do not try to leap across the narrow channel through which the stream rushes and gurgles, because a fall here might well mean the loss of your life. It should be noted that the path below the steps is the most difficult approach to the Strid, because the boulders and stones are always wet and slippery. It is easier and safer to follow the path on the R of the steps and walk down to a prominent Picnic Table which is immediately above the fall. A careful descent to the rocks bordering the stream and a short walk to the L unfolds the finest view of the wild scene. The Strid Woods are now threaded by six Nature Trails, each of them well marked by coloured indicators. Continuing northwards you will soon espy the massive ruin of Barden Tower on the R, and on ascending the hill beyond it you will get a good view on the R of the conspicuous rocks of Simon's Seat, whose slopes on the L fall to the attractive

Plate 168 **Route 38**—Bolton Abbey

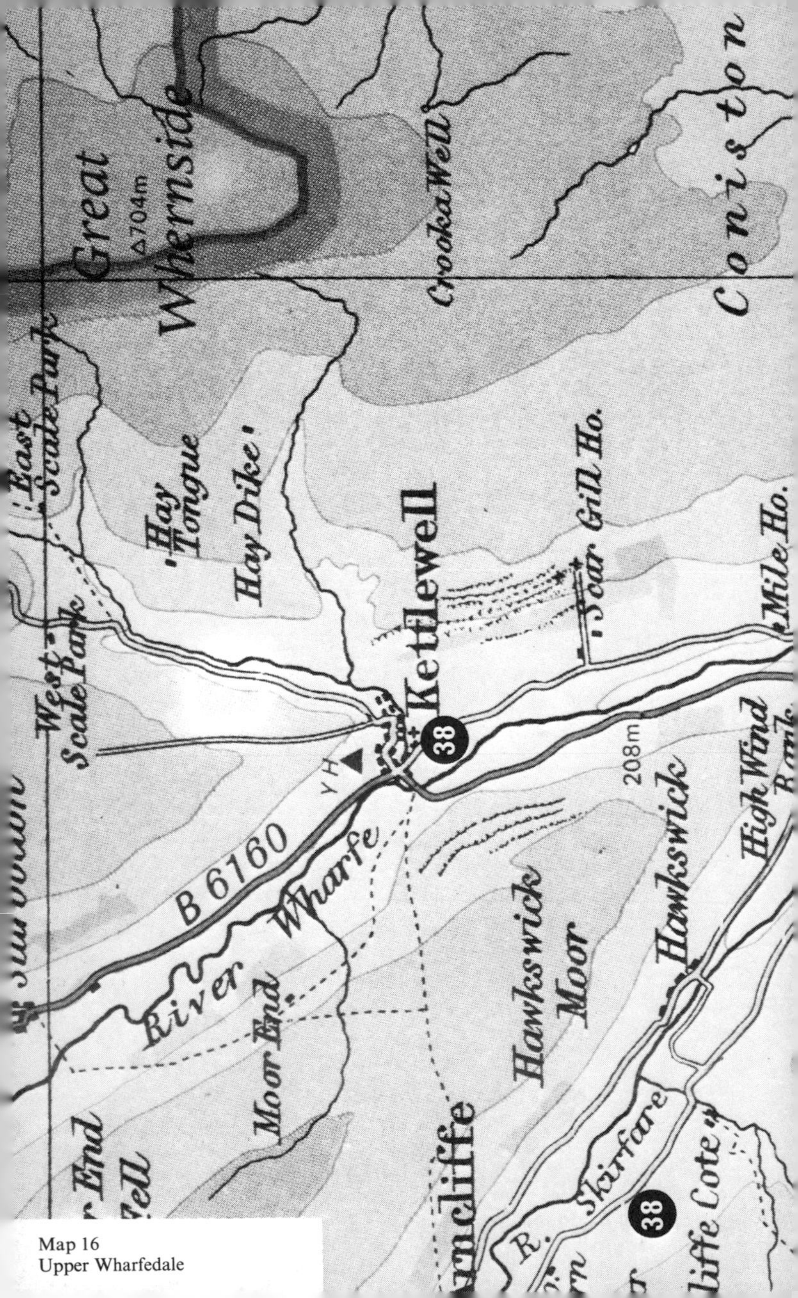

Great Whernside

△704m

Crooka Well

Coniston

'East Scale Park'

'Hay Tongue'

'Hay Dike'

Kettlewell

'Scar Gill Ho.'

Mile Ho.

'West Scale Park'

38

Y H

208m

B 6160

River Wharfe

Hawkswick Moor

Hawkswick

High Wind Bank

Moor End

...cliffe

Skirfare

...cliffe Cote

...End Well

R.

38

Map 16
Upper Wharfedale

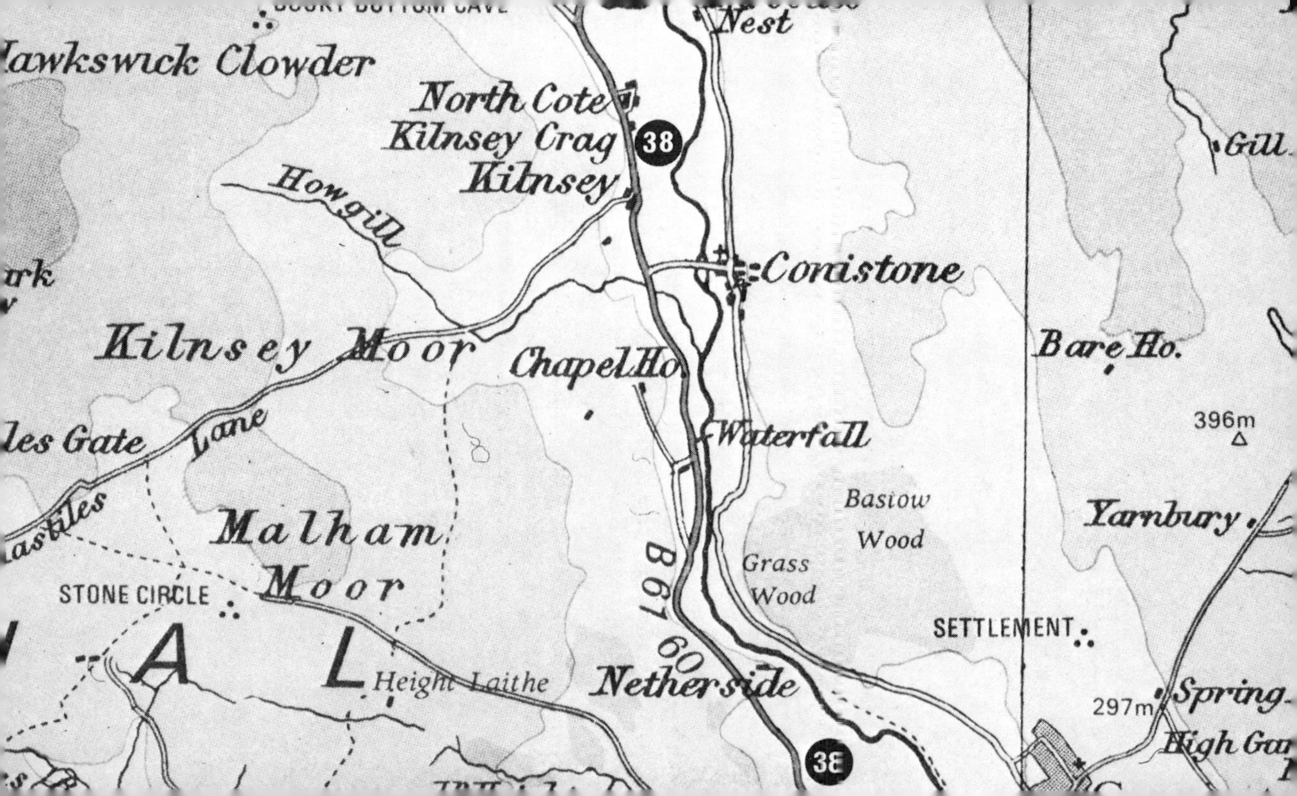

Hawkswuck Clowder

SCORE BOTTOM CAVE

North Cote
Kilnsey Crag
Kilnsey

Howgill

Kilnsey Moor

Les Gate Lane

castles

West

Coniistone

Waterfall

Chapel Ho.

Malham Moor

STONE CIRCLE

Bare Ho.

396m △

Yarnbury

Basiow Wood

Grass Wood

SETTLEMENT

Spring

High Ga

297m

3E

B 61 60

Netherside

Height Laithe

A L

38

village of Appletreewick. Later the descending road reveals Burnsall and its beautiful bridge at the bottom of the hill, and on leaving behind its quaint cottages you will soon encounter Threshfield and Grassington.

The road now rises gently with many undulations as it enters Upper Wharfedale and you will soon perceive ahead the overhanging bulge of Kilnsey Crag. If you are interested in the frontal view of this massive limestone escarpment, park your car and walk across the field opposite which discloses its three sections and tremendous length. Then drive on and if you have time in hand turn to the L at the next fork and continue through the charming valley of Littondale, if only to see Arncliffe, its pump and village green. On returning to the main road you will shortly cross a bridge into Kettlewell, a delightful village standing astride a tuneful beck, and affectionately known to thousands of hikers for its quaint cottages and inns. Driving now along the east bank of the River Wharfe, you will soon reach Starbotton whose cottages are tucked away below the brow of Cam Head, and then Buckden with its houses round the village green and overshadowed by Buckden Pike. Here the road bifurcates, the R branch going over the hills to Aysgarth in Wensleydale, but you should take the L fork and drive on to see the lovely church at Hubberholme, whose Rood Loft is famous and one of the few surviving examples in England. Beyond this hamlet the road is very narrow and passes through Langstrothdale where the cascading stream is in places most picturesque, but you can continue past Oughtershaw and then over the hills to Hawes, taking every care in the ascent and descent of the steep bends en route.

Plate 169 **Route 38**— The Strid

Plate 171 **Route 38**— The approach to Kilnsey Crag

Plate 173 **Route 38**—Frontal view of the Crag

Plate 174 **Route 38**— Arncliffe Green

Plate 175 **Route 38**—Kettlewell

Plate 176 **Route 38**—Hubberholme Church

Plate 177 **Route 38** — The rood loft in Hubberholme Church

Malham Cove

This magnificent limestone outcrop flanks the south side of a grassy hill about a mile from the village of Malham, and is perhaps the most spectacular feature in the Pennines. The cliffs are over 300 feet high and overhang some fourteen feet, where in bygone days a waterfall plunged over the lip of the crags. They form a gigantic semicircle of overhanging precipices, which owing to the action of water and frost are striated vertically, and at the foot of which emerges the infant Aire as a substantial stream. But according to local information this is known as Malham Beck and joins Gordale Beck at Aire Heads which is the real source of the River Aire. Three terraces are festooned across the face of the cliffs; the lowest one may be negotiated easily by anyone with a steady head, but those above it are broken by a gap in the centre and any attempt to traverse them would meet with disastrous results. Swallows and swifts nest on these terraces and haunt the nearby stream and pastures in search of flies. Trees cover the slopes on either side of the chasm and it is well worth while to walk up through them to the summit platform of the Cove, if only to inspect the remarkable Limestone Pavement which will be a revelation. Moreover, the dry bed of the stream which at one time fell over the cliffs is worthy of examination providing always the wayfarer does not venture too near the edge. Photographers will find Malham Cove a most interesting subject and to avoid a chalk-and-soot impression they should arrange to be there with their cameras about 2 p.m. on a sunny day when the favourable lighting then throws into sharp relief every detail of its immense façade.

In recent years rock climbing has developed in Malham Cove, but taking the cliffs as a whole they are the strict preserve of the expert. There are a number of routes on each side of the Central Wall: those on the L include Flake Wall, Original Route, Saplink and the Crab; those on the R are more numerous and include Kirby Wall and Kylin. But the aided

Central Wall was by far the longest and hardest climb, and had for many years received the attention of experts, who despite the protection of the overhang were frequently deterred by heavy rain. However, the successful ascent actually began on August 2nd 1958, when Trevor Peck and Barrie Biven led on alternate days for only twenty or thirty feet and ultimately reached the top after fifty-eight hours of climbing. They started some 100 feet to the R of the stream, went straight up over the shallowest part of the overhang and then L to the lip of the cove. They used twelve pitons and eighty-five ring-screws, and Roger Bacon acted as their assistant. He sharpened twenty-four battered chisels which had been used to make holes in the limestone wall for the rawlplugs etc., each one of which was over one inch deep and took up to half an hour to complete. The total length of this route was 330 feet—some climb!

More recently the Directissima ascent of the Cove had occupied the attention of members of the La Ragni Club for about a year and was successfully accomplished on March 25th, 1967, by Robin Strange and Trevor Briggs. The actual climbing, however, took four to five days when these intrepid cragsmen used Alloy self-drilling anchors of 3,000 lbs breaking strain. Robin tells me this route is good for perhaps 20 years without the danger of the bolts coming out. It starts a few yards to the R of the stream, goes L for only a short distance on the second terrace and thereafter takes a straight line for the overhanging lip of the precipice. More recently, Malham has become the focus of hard, modern free climbing with a vast number of routes created on the lower section of the Central Wall.

Route 39. Drive to Malham and park your vehicle in the car park. Then walk up the narrow walled lane that goes over the hills to Settle, and along which there is no room to park even a small vehicle. In half a mile turn R through a gate in the wall and follow the path which leads straight to the Cove. After passing through the last gate immediately opposite the cliffs, keep to the track beside the beck until you reach the source of the infant Aire at the foot of the frowning precipices. Now climb up through the trees on the R, and on attaining the rim of the Cove bear L and examine the dry bed of the stream, whence proceed to the platform where the astonishingly eroded Limestone Pavement is of particular interest. Finally, go ahead until you encounter the path on the L which descends through the trees, and on reaching ground level stroll back to your car.

In recent years a considerable amount of work has been undertaken by the Yorkshire Dales National Park with a view to facilitating the approach to the Cove. The path descending to the gate facing the Cove is now excellent and a new path at an easier gradient rises to the rim of the Cove, replacing the original track which kept close to the limestone wall. But the approach on the R from the stone bridge over the stream is still extremely difficult and dangerous because the walker has to negotiate safely a sea of boulders which are always wet and slippery, and where a fall might have serious consequences. Surely to complete the existing improvements a path could be made by removing a line of boulders and replacing them with a level path.

Malham Tarn and Gordale Scar

Malham Cove

Plate 178 **Route 39** — Malham Village

Stainforth

Catrigg Force

Cowside Beck

Capon

446m

Up^r Winskill

Cowside

Black Hill

Rocking Stones

Cave

Langcliffe Scar

NT

VICTORIA CAVE

Langcliffe

Back Scar

G

The Shed

Settle Scar

Great Scar

Attermire Scar

Stockdale

42

Settle

C

Stockdale B.

R

EARTHWORK

Stockdale

Rye Hill

Scaleber Force

Scaleber Br.

Force

High

Hunter Bark

Scaleber Beck

388m

Side

atop

Mear Beck

Crake Moor

Otterburn

Map 17
Malham, Gordale and
Attermire

Malham Tarn
Field Centre

Great Close

Tarn
Moss

Malham
Tarn

High
Stony Bank

Streets

Low Tran E

40

Gordale Beck

396m

Prior Raikes

Malham
Lings

Lee Gate Ho.

39

N

A

T

I

O

Ewe
Moor

Malham
Cove

Gordale
Scar

41

Gordale Br.

H

Beck Hall Cott

Friar
Garth

The
Weets

A

Malham

N

V

Acraplaths

Kirkby
Top

219m

Calton
Moor

Out Gang

Kirkby
Malham

Hanlith
Hall

Kirkby Beck

Bark Lathe

Co
M

Moor

Skellands

Dykelands

Scosthrop

Plate 179 **Route 39**—Malham Cove

Plate 180 **Route 39**—Birthplace of the Aire

Plate 181 **Route 39** — Malham Cove from the Rim

Plate 182 **Route 39** — Limestone pavement above the Cove

Malham Tarn

This sheet of water is cradled on the moors less than two miles to the north of the Cove, and owing to its open situation on three sides it is lacking in picturesque appeal. The stream flowing from the Tarn disappears in a 'sink' near the Pennine Way, and was at one time thought to be the source of the Aire which sees the light of day at the base of the Cove. However, it is an excellent centre for Field Study, and Malham Tarn House which is pleasantly situated above the north shore of the tarn has accommodation for a number of keen students.

Route 40. Drive along the narrow road between the cottages encircling the green and at the first fork turn sharp L. The walled lane is steep as it twists uphill and you must keep a sharp lookout for descending traffic at the many sharp bends. On reaching the top of Seaty Hill where the road levels out, stop for a moment and look over the wall on the R which discloses a remarkable display of limestone 'clints', a characteristic feature of the Craven country. Then drive on to the cross roads and park your car on the grass verge, whence walk ahead until you reach the tarn.

Plate 183 **Route 40**—Malham Tarn

Gordale Scar

This spectacular limestone defile is situated about a mile to the north-east of Malham and its narrow entrance is on the grand scale; it is considered by some climbers to be even more striking than its neighbour, Malham Cove. The ravine is S-shaped and its towering mural precipices are more than 200 feet high and on the R overhang considerably. As this is one of the show places in the Pennines, it attracts legions of tourists who, however, can only enter the gorge for a short distance and are brought to a sudden stop on a patch of gravel below the first waterfall. In dry weather there is very little water here and any experienced wayfarer may scramble up the rib on the R which gives access to the upper section of the chasm, but when the beck is in spate it is usually left alone. Beyond it, and high up on the R, is a window through which the upper fall plunges, and in rainy conditions imparts a thunderous clamour to the otherwise quiet gorge. Thence the scenery is less dramatic, and the defile widens out all too soon to emerge on the moor beyond High Stony Bank.

It was not until 1956 that rock climbers gave serious attention to Gordale Scar and began with twenty ascents of the cliffs to the west of the gorge opening. The Face and Cave Routes became popular and the latter required the employment of many karabiners and pitons, and took a full day for its completion. The prodigious impending cliff on the R of the entrance to the Scar proper was first ascended on 8 and 9 June 1963 by J. A. Sumner and D. Sales. These aid climbs were subsequently climbed free, and a variety of others of very high standard were added to Gordale's spectacular repertoire.

Route 41. Mastiles Lane goes over the hills from Malham to Wharfedale and this is the best approach to Gordale Scar. If you go by car follow Route 40 but continue ahead at the fork and park the vehicle in a lay-by on the R. Then walk through the gap in the wall and on reaching the beck follow it into the

Scar. But since the distance is so short it is more delightful to walk all the way and avoid a section of the road by crossing the fields and following the stream as far as the pretty fall known locally as Janet's Foss. Thence the approach is impressive, with limestone outcrops fringing the upper slopes on either hand. But the steep scree slopes hide the chasm itself and give no idea of its dynamic appeal until they almost close upon you and on suddenly rounding the bend on the R you may find yourself overwhelmed by their magnificence. On either side of you they tower into the sky like the gigantic walls of a Titan's workshop and you will probably terminate your walk beneath the first waterfall. Even if you do not scramble up the rib on the R to complete your exploration of the whole gorge, look up on the R and observe the higher fall plunging through a window in the shattered wall of limestone, then amble back to your car.

Plate 184 **Route 41** — The approach to Gordale Scar

Plate 185 **Route 41**—Gordale Scar

Plate 186 **Route 41** Close view of the Overhanging Cliffs

Plate 187 **Route 41**—The Upper and Lower Falls

Attermire

Route 42. These limestone scars are a strange feature of the
Craven Fault. They rise to a height of about 1,350 feet, some
two miles to the north-east of Settle, and may be reached from
the moorland road that connects this busy town with Kirkby
Malham. It leaves the houses as a steep and narrow road, to
level out in just over a mile where a lane on the L goes to
Stockdale Farm. Adjacent to this fork is a space on the L of
the main road where a few cars may be parked. At the second
bend in the farm lane there is a stile in the wall on the L. This
gives easy access to a grassy cart track that rises gently between
High Hill on the L and the conical Sugar Loaf on the R. It is
worth while to ascend the latter as it opens up the whole weird
scene to perfection, with the more massive Warrendale Knotts
on the L and Attermire Scar on the R. Between the two runs
a sketchy diagonal track, first to Attermire Cave and higher up
to Victoria Cave, whence the plateau above may be attained
by a nice scramble. The main crag is a two-tiered cliff which
is a playground for the rock climber. The whole of this area
is patterned by a maze of high stone walls which require careful
negotiation.

Plate 188 Attermire Scar from the Sugar Loaf

Penyghent

2,277 feet   694 metres

Seen from any point in the upper section of Ribblesdale, this mountain presents an attractive appearance with its smooth grassy slopes revealing small outcrops of limestone, and rising gently for some two miles from Plover Hill in the north to its summit in the south where it is rimmed with gritstone crags. The ridge may be attained without difficulty from almost any point, and it is an invigorating and delightful experience to walk south beside the wall to the higher cairn which unfolds a spacious prospect in all directions. The flat, square top of Ingleborough is perhaps the most conspicuous object in the view to the west across the stone-walled enclosures in Ribblesdale. To the R of it rises the smooth ridge of Whernside, the loftiest hill by only a few feet in this part of the Pennines, while Pendle Hill and Bowland Forest are prominent across the moors to the south. In the past decade the above-mentioned outcrop of gritstone has been explored by rock climbers and its broken precipices are gaining favour with these sportsmen.

The countryside in the vicinity is riddled with potholes, and the most interesting ascent of Penyghent takes in two of them to advantage. The first to be encountered is Hull Pot whose vast yawning mouth occupies a depression in the moor at an altitude of 1,250 feet. The cavern is surrounded by a fence and derelict stone wall, doubtless built to prevent sheep falling into it. The roof of this pothole fell in centuries ago and its floor is now fully exposed. It is sixty feet deep, 180 feet long and sixty feet wide, and during a dry spell the beck above it disappears in a 'sink', eventually to emerge from a hole in the side of the pot near its eastern end, whereas in rainy weather most of the water passes over the ground to fall straight into the gash. Quite near at hand and only about 200 yards to the south lies Hunt Pot which is on slightly higher ground than its neighbour at an altitude of 1,300 feet. Here

Plate 189 Penyghent dominates Horton in Ribblesdale

the surface depression is sixty feet wide, but the gullet proper is only fifteen feet long and six feet across at its centre. The ends taper and a jammed boulder at its western extremity enables the wayfarer to stand above the chasm and to look down into its grim depths where the sides are covered with moss, lichens and ferns in great profusion. The hole has two pitches, the first 100 feet and the second sixty feet, and after getting used to the gloom it is possible to pick out the stream taking its single plunge down the first one.

Route 43. Horton in Ribblesdale is the most convenient starting point for the exploration of Penyghent and its adjacent potholes, and its ascent there and back on foot covers a distance of just over seven miles. On approaching the village from Settle you cross a narrow bridge and drive ahead to the car park. Follow the main road and turn R along the Pennine Way up the narrow walled lane which is totally unfit for cars. The lane now winds its way uphill for one and a half miles and ends at a gate beside a building on the R. Continue straight ahead along the grassy cart track until you reach the wire fence protecting the great gash of Hull Pot. The best views of it are from either end, and in wet weather the stream on the north side forms a tumultuous waterfall, sometimes filling the floor of the pothole. Having inspected this remarkable landmark, retrace your steps to the building and turn L through a gate in the wall to follow the Pennine Way in the direction of Penyghent. After the first sharp rise the ground flattens out and is dappled with several shooting butts. About halfway across this level section bear R towards a deep depression in the moor which is fenced and encloses Hunt Pot. You may cross the fence and go down the path to look into the narrow slit in the gritstone, then rejoin the Pennine Way and keep to the old mine track until you attain the dip in the ridge ahead. Here turn R and follow the wall to the cairn on Penyghent.

This is a superb situation for lunch, and after resting awhile continue south until the precipitous belt of gritstone is encountered. If you are an experienced climber you will find your way down the face of the outcrop, but otherwise it is safer to bear L and walk down the side of the escarpment until easier ground is reached, whence bear R round the southern end of your mountain until you pick up the beck falling into Hunt Pot, and so back to the lane and your car.

Penyghent is the first of the renowned 'Three Peaks' and is followed in these pages by a description of the other two— Ingleborough and Whernside. To traverse them all in one day is the ambition of many keen walkers and in favourable weather they make a first class expedition, allowing ample time for leisurely viewing the scenery, photography and refreshment. This is the scene of the famous Three Peaks Race, which covers 24 miles and 4,500 feet of ascent and descent. At the time of writing the record was held by Hugh Seymour of Kendal who completed the circuit in 2 hours 49.13 minutes. Over-heavy use of the path in consequence of its popularity has required improvements on some sections of the route.

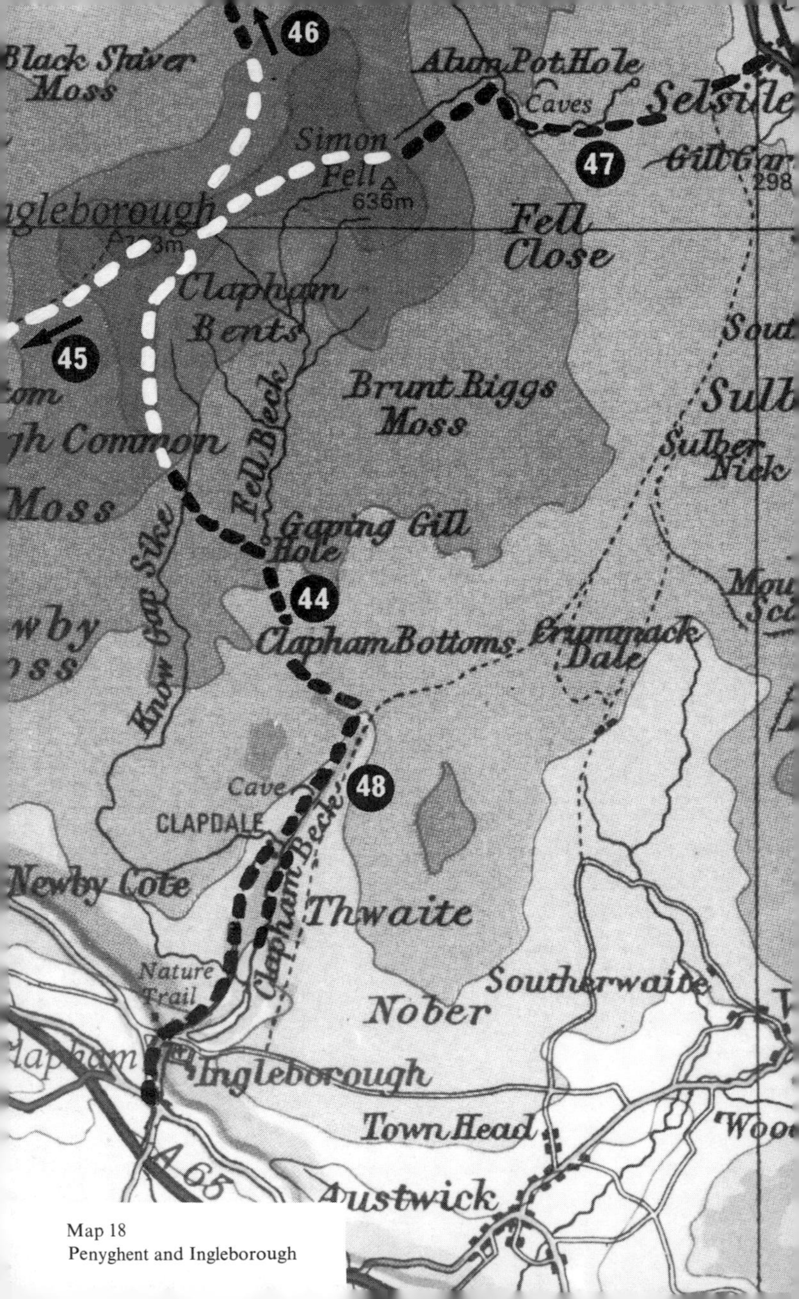

46

Black Shiver
Moss

Alum Pot Hole

Caves

Selside

47

Simon
Fell
△
636m

Gill Gar

298

Ingleborough

3m

Fell
Close

Clapham
Bents

Brunt Riggs
Moss

Sout

Sulb

45

Sulber
Nick

gh Common

Moss

Gaping Gill
Hole

Crummack
Dale

Mou
Sca

44

Clapham Bottoms

wby

oss

Know Gap Sike

Fell Beck

48

Cave
CLAPDALE

Clapham Beck

Thwaite

Newby Cote

Southerwaite

Nature
Trail

Nober

V

Clapham

Ingleborough

Town Head

Woo

A 65

Austwick

Map 18
Penyghent and Ingleborough

Scale

Top

River Ribble

Hull Pot Beck

Pen-y-ghent Si...

Horton Moor

Hull Pot

Hunt Pot

...ow Moor

New Houses

43

Pen-y-ghen...
89...

Cave

Horton Scur

43

Harber

Hall

Gavel Rigg

Fawce... Moo...

Brackenbottom

Horton in Ribblesdale

Dub Cote Scar

Dale Head

Crag Hill

on

Dub Cote

Newland Ho.

Y

Higher Studfold

Silverda...

Arcow

Studfold

...redale

Helwith Br.

End Ho.

Moor Head Lane

Silverdale Road

Ne...

Swarth Moor

Sherwood Ho.

Sannet...

...dale Ho.

B 6...

Plate 100. Part of Sgwd Henrhyd. *a* post-swell

Plate 191 **route 43**—Hunt Pot—a dry spell

Plate 192 **Route 43**—Upper band of gritstone

Plate 193 **Route 43**—Ingleborough from the Lower Band

Ingleborough

2,372 feet   723 metres

This mountain is one of the great landmarks of the Pennines and dominates the vast moorland triangle based upon Ingleton and Settle. The summit consists of a square, almost level gritstone cap which is well seen from many of the fells to the north and east, and from the roads threading the Bowland, Pendle and Brontë country to the south, while it is a prominent eminence in the Pennine skyline when observed on a clear day from the distant Lakeland Fells to the west. Its flattish top carries four cairns, of which the highest and largest overlooks the extensive, walled landscape to the south-west, but its chief interest is that as one of the Craven Highlands it stands upon the immense belt of limestone which is riddled with potholes, not only on the massif itself, but also on the adjacent hills and dales. There are four routes to its summit which start respectively from Clapham, Ingleton, Chapel-le-Dale and Selside, and any two of them may be used by the walker for the ascent and descent providing he does not wish to return to the chosen starting point. The best combined route begins at Clapham and takes in Gaping Gill on the ascent, and continues over Simon Fell to take in Alum Pot on the descent to Selside. This is the most interesting route for the strong walker, and without deviations covers a distance of just over eight miles.

Gaping Gill is the finest pothole in Britain and receives the waters of Fell Beck, whose tributaries have their source on the slopes of Ingleborough and Simon Fell. In some two miles the stream reaches limestone and begins to sink in its bed, but the unabsorbed water flows into Gaping Gill at an altitude of 1,300 feet. The pothole is roughly circular in shape and large enough to take a horse and cart without touching its grim, fern-decorated, vertical walls which are not protected in any way. The shaft is 340 feet deep and at 190 feet there is a notorious ledge, below which the Great Hall opens out. This

353

is the main chamber with a floor space of half an acre and one of the largest in the world. Measuring 500 feet long, ninety feet wide and 110 feet high, it could contain one of our smaller cathedrals. Connected with it is a complex system of passages and deeper potholes extending some 3,110 yards underground, which together with the 900 yards of Ingleborough Cave in the same series, total nearly two and a half miles of caverns with underwater links to others. A glance into this yawning chasm should be sufficient to warn off would-be adventurers. It was ascended by Roger Baxter Jones in a dry season.

Alum Pot is perhaps the next most interesting pothole, and lies on the eastern slopes of Simon Fell, above the hamlet of Selside at an altitude of 1,125 feet. Its ugly mouth is surrounded by trees and protected by a stone wall and fence through which flows the stream to fall in a single plunge of 210 feet. The total depth of the chasm is 292 feet, but the shaft is blocked by a gigantic boulder known as the Bridge. Three hundred feet of rope is required for its direct descent, but if the side passage known as Long Churn is used, half this length only is needed.

The Norber Erratics lie on the south-eastern flanks of this massif and should be seen by all who are interested in geology. They are a heterogeneous collection of Silurian boulders weighing up to 20 tons, many standing on limestone pedestals and deposited in the Ice Age. The key to their discovery is Austwick, which may be conveniently reached from either Settle or Clapham. At the northern end of the village a narrow walled 'no through road' branches off to the L, and after crossing Thwaite Lane descends sharply to a gate on the L. A small car could be turned here, but a large one should be driven up the next hill at the top of which there is ample space to turn round. Park the car at the gate and walk up a steep grassy slope to some trees on the brow of the moor; go forward and cross a high wall which encloses the Erratics. They lie in confusion on the extensive grassy shelf below the prominent limestone scar and one of the best

Plate 195 Morning mist clearing from Ingleborough

examples, illustrated in these pages, will be found at the extremity of the collection.

Tourists who do not wish to undertake the ascent of Ingleborough should at least visit Ingleton Falls. This involves an enchanting walk at an easy gradient through the woods, and the stream is crossed frequently by footbridges near some of the most famous falls, although by far the most beautiful of them, Thornton Force, is on the open moorland above.

Route 44. Drive to Clapham and leave the vehicle in the car park. Pass through a sawmill and pay a small fee to walk through the delightful grounds of Ingleton House. But if you prefer a loftier approach turn up the lane on the R beyond the mill which skirts Raygill Plantation, and on reaching Clapdale Farm take the path on the R which merges with the former route. This walk is charming and while passing through the woods you will perceive the placid waters of the lake on your R, and thereafter be accompanied by the water music of Cave Beck which cascades through a ravine low down on the R. On emerging from the leafy canopy cross a stile to enter a verdant pasture which leads to Ingleborough Cave on the L. This is situated at the base of a massive outcrop of limestone at an altitude of 900 feet, and if you have time in hand it is worth while to take the local guide and explore its half mile of passages where numerous stalactites and stalagmites decorate its walls, ceiling and floor, and of which the most picturesque are the Jockey Cap, Ladies' Throne, Ring of Bells and Elephant Legs. Just beyond its entrance you may look into the dark hole where the stream from the subterranean passages of Gaping Gill reaches the light of day. Continue your walk through the narrowing dale, which on bending to the L reveals the imposing ravine of Trow Gill. Centuries ago this probably carried off the water from the eastern flank of Ingleborough and on first acquaintance seems to afford no exit, but by carefully ascending the loose scree and boulders you will find a narrow opening which gives access to the moor. Now follow the path beside the stone wall on your L

Plate 196 One of the Norber Erratics

which in due course crosses it when open ground is reached. Keep to the indistinct track in the direction of Ingleborough to the north and in passing look into the entrance to Bar Pot on the L which is the easiest descent to the main chamber of Gaping Gill when Fell Beck is in spate, then go ahead until you discover Gaping Gill in a moorland depression which is protected on this side by a wire fence. Walk down the track on the R to look into its grim depths and remember that wet limestone is very slippery and unsafe if you are wearing rubber soles. Return to the moor and, leaving the hole on your R, cross the boggy ground in a north-westerly direction and ascend the southern spur of your mountain. The going is steep until you reach the grassy ridge, whence bear R for a conspicuous sheepfold which reveals the summit of Ingleborough to the north. Now cross the intervening boggy ground to gain the track on the R of its flat top where a well-built shelter stands in its centre. This is surmounted by an Indicator which was erected by the Ingleton Fell Rescue Team to commemorate the Coronation of Her Gracious Majesty Queen Elizabeth II, on June 2nd, 1955. It is made of copper plate and its pointers mark accurately all the main landmarks in the encircling panorama.

Plate 197 Thornton Force

Plate 198 **Route 44**—Potholers pass Ingleborough Cave

Plate 199 **Route 44**—Trow Gill

Plate 200 **Route 44**—Potholers cross the stile to the moor

Plate 201 **Route 44**—Fell Beck runs into Gaping Gill

Plate 202 **Route 44**—Close-up of Gaping Gill Hole

Plate 203 **Route 44** — Ingleborough from the Sheepfold

Whernside

Plate 204 **Route 44**— Hikers rest on the summit shelter

Plate 205 **Route 44**—Looking across the Dale to Whernside

Route 45. Start this walk from Ingleton and follow the Hawes road to the top of the village. On reaching open ground turn R and keep to the cart track which rises gradually to Crina Bottom. Thence follow the path in a direct line for the summit of Ingleborough, making your way carefully over the slippery limestone clints, loose blocks and screes, but the real collar work begins when you reach the gritstone cap. This is steep but not difficult, and on attaining the summit walk over to the shelter and rest after the ardours of the ascent.

Route 46. Drive up B6255 in the direction of Hawes and on reaching the Hill Inn at Chapel-le-Dale ask the owner if you may park your car in the yard at the back. Then pass through a gate on the L and follow the wall until you attain the limestone shelf, whence make your way step by step across it and finally ascend the last steep band of gritstone to tread the flat summit of Ingleborough.

Route 47. Drive up B6479 to Selside and after passing the hamlet turn L along a cart track in the direction of Alum Pot, which may be identified by a plantation on the higher ground below Simon Fell. This track is rough, and if you have any respect for your car you may prefer to park it at the point where the surface begins to deteriorate. Otherwise you can drive on for another half mile and then walk a short distance to the Pot, but do not venture beyond the fence to look into the hole unless you have a very steady head. Now walk over to Long Churn but do not enter it without a torch, as in the darkness you may stumble and sprain an ankle. Then cross Borrins Moor and make for Simon Fell where the last section of the climb is steep. On attaining the crest of the ridge turn L and follow the the rim of the coombe, and later R up the spur which terminates on the flat summit of your mountain.

NOTE. Alum Pot is on private ground and a small fee is now payable by all visitors.

Plate 206 **Route 45** — The view on attaining the summit

Plate 207 **Route 47**—Alum Pot from Long Churn

White Scar Cave

This cavern penetrates the lower western flank of
Ingleborough and its entrance is on the R of B6255, just over
two miles to the north-east of Ingleton. It is a Master Cave
and differs from those already described in these pages,
because it can be entered at its point of debouchure which is
the main drainage channel for over thirty subsidiary streams,
some of which have only recently been explored. The original
entrance was sealed by a pool whose surface touched the roof,
but it was drained by C. F. D. Long who was thus responsible
for the opening up of the extensive system of caves beyond. At
this point the limestone was subsequently excavated for some
250 yards as far as the First Waterfall where the natural
caverns begin. While the system rises gently from the entrance,
its remarkable feature is that the roof is flat and unbroken as
far as Swift's Lake where the fissure towers overhead for over
200 feet. The passage open to the public is half a mile long,
and much of its floor is covered with boards under which some
of the water drains away. Electric lighting provides adequate
illumination for the examination of each feature. I was given
every facility by the owner at the time, Mrs Mabel Sharp who
was also an experienced mountaineer, and was shown through
the cave by one of her assistant guides, Crispin Fryer, a student
from Sheffield University.

Route 48. Drive up to the cave entrance and park your car in
the space below the house and its adjacent refreshment hut.
Take a guide and enter the excavated portion where at the
first bend to the L you will notice a strong Flood Door, with
beyond it a high water mark on an electric light bulb. You
will soon hear the thunderous reverberations of the First
Waterfall and after climbing some steps you may enter the
chamber on the L to see it. The Natural Cave now opens out
and displays many interesting and beautiful features that will
be pointed out by your guide. Among them are the Second
Waterfall, Long's Gallery, Budda, the Rippling Cascade, the

Indian Totem Pole and finally the White Stalagmite beyond which the Barrier halts further progress to the tourist, but if you happen to be an experienced speleologist permission may be granted for the exploration of a further two and a half miles of passages.

Plate 208 **Route 48**—Budda

Whernside

2,415 feet   736 metres

This mountain is the highest in this region of the Pennines,
and rises to the north-west of Ribblehead Station on B6255.
As a long grassy ridge that slopes up gently from the south, it
presents its most imposing appearance when seen from
Ribblehead, but exhibits no dynamic features that will draw the
climber. A high stone wall runs along its entire crest and the
actual summit is marked by an O.S. Triangulation Station.
The ascent presents no difficulties whatsoever and it makes an
invigorating morning or afternoon walk. But since it is
surrounded by many walled enclosures a zig-zag course is
necessary for those who do not like to cross them, as the gates
from one field to another are not in line with the direct
approach to the ridge. Nevertheless, on a clear day Whernside
is a splendid coign of vantage, and reveals to the east and
south some fine views of Penyghent and Ingleborough, while
to the north-west it opens up a striking prospect of the hills
about Sedbergh.

Route 49. Drive north along B6255, and just before you reach
the Hill Inn above the hamlet of Chapel-le-Dale turn L
through a gate and continue along the winding paved road in
the direction of Bruntscar. Park your vehicle on the grass
verge before reaching the farm, and then walk towards it but
turn R to pass through a gate giving access to the pastures.
Unless you are prepared to take a direct line across the many
stone walls, you must now work out the problem of locating
the various gates in the direction of your peak, and on passing
through the last of them go forward towards Combe Scar on
the skyline. In due course you will reach a derelict cross wall
and this is the key to the stiff ascent of the slippery grass ridge
ahead. Keep Combe Scar on your L and later pass a collection
of boulders on your R, above which you will soon encounter
the stone wall on top of the ridge. Now turn R and follow it to

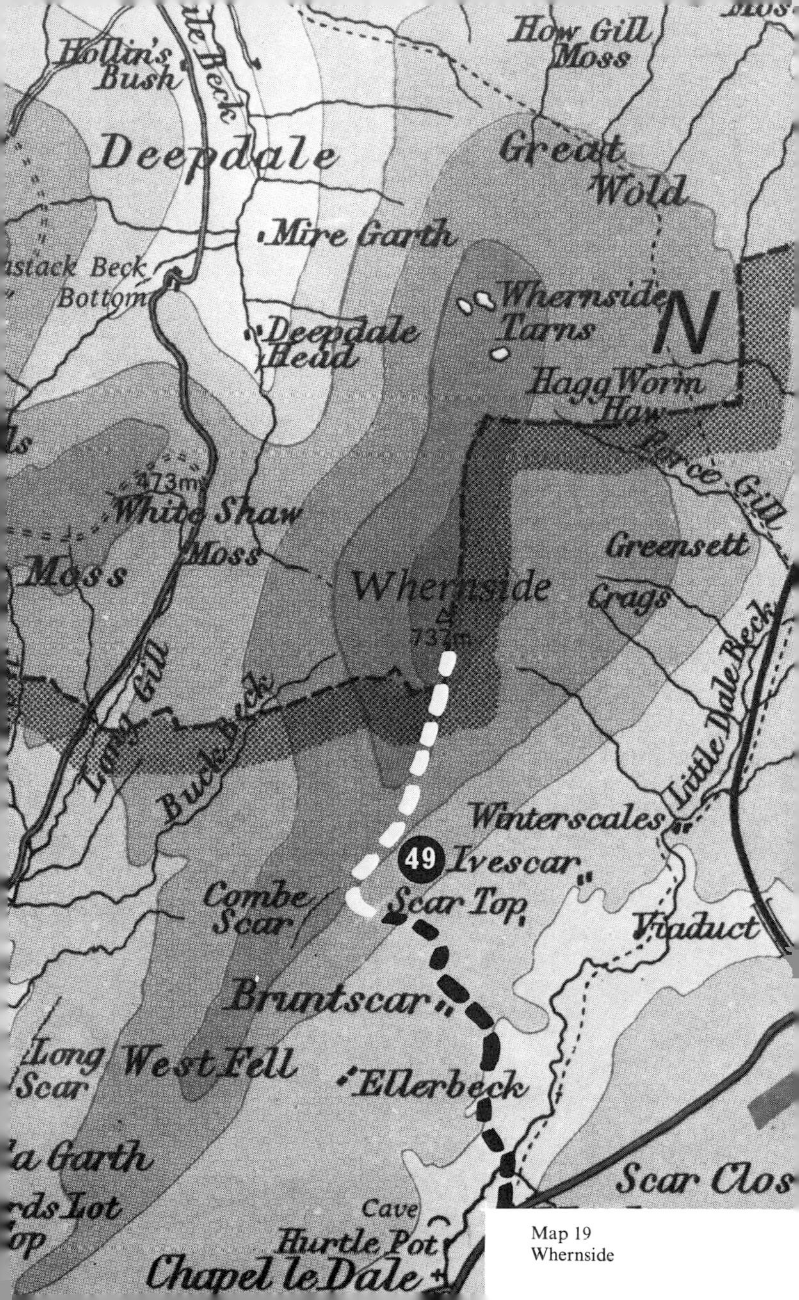

Map 19
Whernside

the inconspicuous summit, noting on the R the famous railway viaduct far below, and on your return the fine elevation of Ingleborough.

Plate 209 **Route 49** — Starting point for the ascent

Plate 210 **Route 49**—The summit ridge

Penyghent

Plover Hill

Plate 211 **Route 49**—Penyghent and the viaduct from the ridge

Plate 212 **Route 49** — Ingleborough seen across the Dale

Wensleydale

This lovely Yorkshire dale deeply penetrates the Pennines and stretches almost due west from Leyburn to the Moorcock Inn, whence it bends to the north and ends on the Cumbria boundary below Ure Head. It is threaded by the River Ure and has a total length of over 25 miles. On either side it is graced by a number of subsidiary dales, all of which bring their quota of streams to swell the Ure, and by Semer Water, which is usually considered to be the largest natural lake in the West Riding. The beautiful scenery of Wensleydale reveals none of the characteristics of those already described, whereas it excels in individual scenes of waterplay and in charming villages whose cottages are tastefully arranged round village greens, both of which are without compare. The dale takes its name from the village of Wensley which is internationally famous for its cheese, but this industry has spread to such an extent that the cheese is now made by farmers throughout the dale.

Route 50. Since it is possible that you may be touring the Pennines from south to north, you will approach Wensleydale from Wharfedale by the picturesque road that goes over the hills from Buckden. In this event you will first encounter the romantic village of West Burton which stands at the entrance to the subsidiary Walden Dale. Here you should park your car and wander round its exquisite combination of cottage, shop and inn, all of them delightfully placed round a green whose grass might well have originated in Cumbria, and where peace and contentment reign over its 1820 Monument and well preserved stocks. Now drive on to join A684 which is the main highway through Wensleydale, and on reaching it turn L and later R at the inn to view the splendour of the waterplay of the River Ure. Known as Aysgarth Forces, they form the most attractive section of the river and look their best when the stream is in spate. You may view the Upper Fall from the

Rowantree Park

Castle Bolton

CAS

Castle Bank

Lo...

Re...

High Thoresby

Hollin Ho.

Swin...

...by Force

Sorrelsykes Park

West Bolton

Wensleydale

Manor Ho.

160m

+ Ch.

Nature Trail

S

YH

Carperby

Bear Park

Ballowfield

Greenhaw Hut

Carperby Moor

Locker Tarn

Blue Scar

Ivy Scar

Woodhall Park

50

Aysgarth

50

Woodhall Moor

...iggin

Heugh

Nappa Scar

Hall

Nappa

Worton

S

A 684

W

Thornton Rust

...ton Rust

NT

Riggs Ho.

50

Map 20
Wensleydale

Haw Head
Littleburn
Side Head
Blind Syke
Heck Brow
Bishop Dale
B 6160
West Burton
50
Forelands
Cote
Burton Moor
Newbiggin
Bishopdale Beck
Lane Ho.
Harland Hill
536m
Rookery
New Gill Ho.
Ribba Hall
Myres Garth
Beck
Cross Ho.
White Row
Gammer Moor
Hargill Ho.
Haw Ho.
Dewersit Moss
Walden Moor
Bishopdale Edge
Bridge End
Dovescar
Fleemis
Gill

first bridge and then drive on to leave your vehicle in the car park. Now walk along the nearby path that passes through the trees on the north bank of the stream and observe the single plunge of the Middle Fall, whence continue a short distance and descend the bank to revel in the magnificence of the Lower Fall. This passes through a narrow opening in the trees, descends over a series of ledges to finally widen out until it becomes a succession of glittering cascades. Returning to your car, you drive on to Carperby whose village cross is a prominent feature, and then on to Castle Bolton which stands on the northern slopes of the dale. Park your car and inspect the castle which dominates the scene hereabouts; it was built in the fourteenth century and was the home and stronghold of the Scropes. Now drive back to the main highway and turn R to pass through Aysgarth on the way to Bainbridge. But before reaching this village you will see a signpost on the L for Semer Water, where you may elect to drive over the narrow hill road to see this lake and continue by way of Countersett to Bainbridge. This is another village of enchantment with shady trees and cottages arranged at intervals round the green, at whose extensive centre stands the stocks. Continuing westwards again, you will soon run into Hawes, and its charm is enchanced by the adjacent villages of Appersett on the one hand and by Gayle on the other: the houses of the latter standing on the edge of a wide stream which cascades over broad ledges, but which in a dry spell are the playground of its children.

To end your exploration of Wensleydale, you should visit Hardrow Force which lies in a deep depression on its northern slopes. On payment of a small fee, you pass through the parlour of the Green Dragon Inn and walk along the narrow dale beside Fossdale Gill, and on reaching the last bend are confronted by the Fall. In one uninterrupted drop of nearly 100 feet, it plunges from the rim of limestone which overhangs the receding banks of soft shale. If you are an adventurous wayfarer you may walk close behind it and secure an unusual view of the ravine through its myriads of luminous drops of water. The approach, however, is prosaic and lacks the romantic aspect of the upper gorge because a bandstand stands beside the stream and in the centre of a green.

The dale now becomes wilder and is overlooked by the satellites of Great Shunner Fell on the north, and by Widdale Fell on the south. From the Moorcock Inn it has a barren aspect, and on swinging round to the north beneath the great bulk of East Baugh Fell, enters perhaps its most desolate stretches, which in a few miles end at the Cumbria boundary.

An interesting addition to this route is to drive westwards from the Moorcock Inn along the delightful stretches of Garsdale, and on approaching Sedbergh turn sharp R and enter the beautiful Rawthey Valley. This is hemmed in on the L by the Howgills and on the R by Baugh Fell, and on reaching the Cross Keys Temperance Hotel park the car beyond it. Towering on the western skyline is the Calf, 2220 feet high and dominating the Howgills, with below it the imposing ring of Cautley Crag with Cautley Spout immediately on its R. Those who wish to take a closer view may cross the footbridge below the lay-by and follow the path to the falls. They are situated in a narrow cleft in the green hillside, and when the four cascades are in spate they make an attractive display.

Plate 213 **Route 50**— West Burton village green

Plate 214 **Route 50** — Aysgarth Force — upper fall

Plate 215 **Route 50** — The middle fall

Plate 216 **Route 50** —The cascading lower fall

Plate 217 **Route 50**—Castle Bolton

Plate 218 **Route 50**—Storm brewing over Semer Water

Plate 219 **Route 50**—Stocks on Bainbridge village green

Plate 220 **Route 50**—Hardrow Force

Plate 221 **Route 50**—Cautley Crag and Spout

Butter Tubs

The pass familiarly known by this name is the connecting link
between the upper section of Wensleydale and Swaledale to
the north. It carries a well-paved road which, after crossing wild
expanses of moorland reaches the col between Great Shunner
Fell on the west and Lovely Seat on the east, thereafter to
descend past the 'Tubs' and eventually to Swaledale.
Motorists who do not know the significance of the name of
this pass might well slip past the 'Tubs' with scarcely a glance
at them. They consist of a few infant potholes varying in
depth from perhaps twenty to sixty feet, and contrary to the
usual smooth walls of these chasms, they have peculiar fluted
sides with ribbed flat-topped pinnacles, all of which are worn
away by water trickling down their soft limestone. They are
grouped together on the L of the road, which runs on the edge
of steep scree slopes and may be located opposite a rather frail
wooden fence on the R above the scree.

Route 51. Drive north from Hawes until you reach the road
connecting Appersett with Askrigg, then turn L and later R
which will bring you to High Shaw at the foot of Butter Tubs.
After leaving behind the last cottage in this hamlet the road
steepens and on reaching the open moor you will notice the
poles driven into the ground on either side which act as route
indicators in severe winters, when the pass is snowbound. On
the L you will observe the flattish summit of Great Shunner
Fell and on the R the rough slopes of Lovely Seat, and after
passing the watershed it is advisable to reduce speed if you
wish to look into the 'Tubs' on your L. Thereafter the road
sweeps down the hillside in wide curves and with splendid
views of the spacious valley below, until finally you drop
down into Swaledale.

Map 21
Wensleydale and Butter Tubs

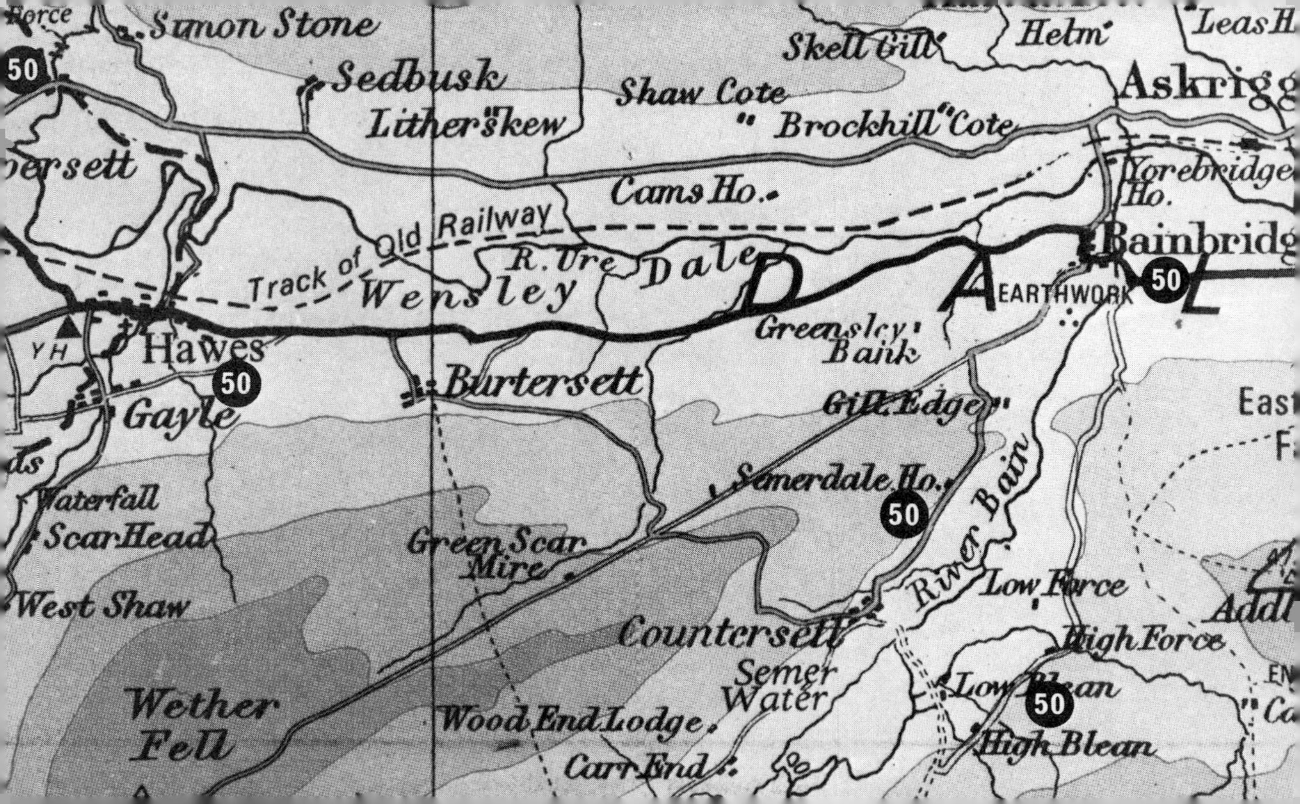

Simon Stone
Sedbusk
Litherskew
Skell Gill
Helm
Shaw Cote
Brockhill Cote
Askrigg
Cams Ho.
Yorebridge Ho.
Track of Old Railway
R. Ure
Wensley Dale
Bainbridge
EARTHWORK
Hawes
YH
Gayle
Burtersett
Greensley Bank
Gill Edge
Semerdale Ho.
River Bain
Low Force
High Force
Waterfall
Scar Head
Green Scar Mire
West Shaw
Countersett
Semer Water
Wether Fell
Wood End Lodge
Carr End
High Blean
50

Plate 222 **Route 51**—Butter Tubs

Swaledale

This Yorkshire dale is one of the least frequented in the Pennines and its upper reaches are remote, wild and little known. It extends westwards from Richmond to Thwaite, bends to the north as far as Keld and then takes a northwesterly course to end at Lambs Moss on the lofty Cumbria boundary. But, strangely enough its terminal stretches are known as Birkdale, and although B6270 accompanies the River Swale for much of its course, the stream passes to the east of Kisdon, between Muker and Keld, while the road swings round the western flank of this hill. The river has its source on the slopes of High Pike and receives water from many subsidiary dales throughout its long course; it is also fed by the beck from Birkdale Tarn, the only sheet of water in the dale and situated to the north of the road some three miles to the west of Keld. The total length of Swaledale is about twenty-eight miles and much of it is barren and lacking in picturesque appeal. The road beyond Muker is narrow and sinuous and has little to offer the motorist, whereas the surrounding country is ideal tramping ground for the tough walker who will enjoy not only the spacious landscape and particularly the glen scenery in the vicinity of Crackpot Hall, but also the music of the many cataracts and waterfalls that grace the river. Moreover, this region is famous for its sheep which are tough and hardy, so much so that they thrive at elevations and under weather conditions that would kill many other breeds. Each of the widely distributed farms in this dale and its subsidiaries have special identification marks for their flocks of sheep, and are contained in a volume known as the Swaledale 'Smit-book'. Finally, Swaledale was at one time the prolific source of minerals, mainly lead, and the workings and tunnels were extensively distributed, some of which may still be found in rifts on the hillsides.

Route 52. The road from Richmond to Muker is outside the scope of this work, and you will therefore reach Swaledale from Butter Tubs as described in the last monograph. On reaching B6270 turn R for Muker whose cottages are clustered round the church which completely dominates the village. Years ago it was the local centre of the lead mining industry, when workers had small farms in the vicinity, of which many have been pulled down or left in ruins. Now drive back along B6270 and observe the charming situation of Thwaite at the foot of the steep slopes of Kisdon, and later the cottages that constitute the hamlet of Keld. Half a mile beyond it drive over the bridge on the R and ascend the steep, narrow hill road which is well paved and has a double S-bend at a gradient of one in three. Thence it runs high above the stream and after passing the few cottages of West Stonesdale you ascend gradually across the bleak, open moorland, eventually to reach Tan Hill which is reputed to be the highest inn in Britain. This is a desolate spot and in a severe winter is isolated from time to time, but it should never be cold indoors as coal of poor quality can be obtained from the disused King's Colliery, less than a mile away.

There are two alternative routes for the continuation of your drive: one of them is to take the L fork at Tan Hill for Barras and to later join A66(T) for Barnard Castle and Teesdale; the other is to drive back to B6270 and follow Swaledale to the Cumbria boundary, and thence over Tailbridge Hill for Kirby Stephen when the run downhill reveals a magnificent vista to the north.

Map 22
Swaledale and
Tan Hill

Plate 223 **Route 52**—Muker

Plate 224 **Route 52** — Tan Hill Inn — the highest in England

Teesdale

The River Tees rises on the southern flank of Cross Fell in
Cumbria and for a few miles forms the boundary between it
and Teesdale. After it has been joined by Crookham Beck, its L
bank enters the county of Durham, but when Maize Beck flows
into it below Caldron Snout, its R bank passes into Yorkshire,
and it remains the dividing line between these two counties for
the rest of its course until it enters the North Sea. The river is
some eighty-five miles in length and in the early part of its
course passes through some of the wildest country in the
Pennines where hills and bleak moorland afford scenes of
desolate grandeur. At Caldron Snout it forms a series of rapids
and flows over a bed of hard rock consisting of black basalt.
Trees soon appear to soften the barren landscape, and at High
Force it provides one of the finest falls in England. Here both
evergreens and deciduous trees fringe its banks in profusion,
and on entering pastoral country its scenery becomes gentler
and more picturesque. At Middleton-in-Teesdale it assumes
more stately proportions and then passes the town of Barnard
Castle, followed by Eggleston and Rokeby. At Winton the
valley opens out and the broad river meanders across the rich
plain below Darlington, to become finally a waterway of great
commercial importance where the ports of Stockton-on-Tees,
Thornaby-on-Tees and Middlesbrough form the outlet for the
vast industries of North Yorkshire.

Teesdale is closely associated with Queen Elizabeth I, for
she spent much of her girlhood at Streatlam Castle, where her
family estates extended for miles on both banks of the river,
and included Mickle Fell, the highest peak in Yorkshire,
together with grouse moors and farmlands. The castle has
been held by one line since the twelfth century, though
heiresses have carried it by marriage to Trayne, Bowes and
Lyon.

Teesdale is a more spacious valley than any of the others
previously described in this volume, and its finest scenery
begins at Barnard Castle and ends at Cross Fell. But for the

motorist who likes to walk only a short distance from his car, a few only of its many interesting features can be seen, although the desolation of its immense moorland landscape may be observed on either hand all the way along the gradually rising B6277, where the road attains an altitude of nearly 2,000 feet before falling to Alston. Hence, this dale is the valued preserve of the strong walker, who must cover tremendous distances over remote and often boggy moorland if he is not only to see its hidden beauty, but also to enjoy its profound solitude. The longest, most arduous and repaying route starts at High Force, and following the Pennine Way, passes Langdon Beck, Caldron Snout, Maize Beck and High Cup Nick on the way to Dufton, a distance of nearly twenty miles.

Route 53. As you drive up to Barnard Castle you will observe its beautiful situation on the steep northern banks of the Tees, together with the graceful mediaeval bridge spanning the river, and the picturesque old houses adjoining it, which are dominated by the grand ruin where the Balliol Family were nurtured. The castle is the principal scene of Sir Walter Scott's *Rokeby*, and is worth seeing, as is also the Bowes Museum, built in 1892 in the French chateau style. This is reputed to have cost £100,000, and houses a private collection of porcelain, pictures and tapestries. The industry of Barnard Castle was formerly that of carpet making, first in the hand loom and then in the factory, while the tanning of leather and manufacture of shoe thread were also important.

Proceeding north-westwards you pass the charming villages of Lartington, Cotherstone and Ronaldkirk on the way to Middleton-in-Teesdale which is a good centre not only for its river scenery but also for walks over its adjacent hills. Three miles further along B6277 you should park your car and turn down a path to the L which leads to Winch Bridge for the view of its narrow gorge, and if you follow the river upstream beyond the woods where the country is more open you will see it coming down over a wide stretch of basalt to form

qe Ho.

ale Ho.

Blea

Broadleys Gate

Force Garth

The High
Force

R.
Groo

Fie
Het

53

Howgill
Ho.

Bowlees

B 6277

Wynch B

53

Ore
Carr

Holwick
Lo.

N

Holwick

Holwick
Fell

Green Fell
End

oss

Rowton Beck

Par.

Millstone How
Hill

Rotten
Rig

Green Fell

Buck C

Riggs

535m
△

Bink
Moss

618m
△

LUNE MOOR

Low Bink
Moss

ock
ake

Map 23
Teesdale

Pikestone Brow

Coldberry

Mine (Disused)

Mine (Disused)

△ 565m

△ 529m

Hardberry Hill

Chub Gill

Monk's Moo

Raven Hills

gin

kets Fm

Middle Side

Auk Side

Hudeshope Beck

Cocklands

Co

Dent Bank

Middleton in Teesdale

Stotley

West Stotley

River Tees

D

53

A   L   E

B

E

sthwaite

Lonton

sthwaite

mmon

Pennine Way

Laithkirk

Mickleton

er Fell

△ 481m

Bowbank

lebow

East Park

Thringarth

Stake Hill

dale

Bail Hill

G

pe Beck

3m

burn

pe Beck

glittering cascades and placid pools that make an attractive subject for your camera. A mile further on you will come to the hotel facing the entrance to High Force where you should park your car and walk down the woodland path to view it. The fall is perhaps the river's most spectacular feature, for here it passes between two great bastions of basalt, and when in spate forms a second and smaller cascade on the R. Should you wish to view the fall from above, you may do so by climbing some steps on the R and scrambling over the adjoining rocks and boulders. Here the scene upstream is one of desolation backed by high moorland, whereas the view downstream through the narrow gorge is a sylvan prospect of surprising beauty. Photographers will have noticed that High Force is an unsatisfactory subject as it faces the north-east and is therefore poorly illuminated. Even on an early summer morning the sunlight does not catch the rock wall on the L of the fall, but only skims across the bastion on the R. On the contrary, a good picture may be taken from the top of the fall looking downstream, which is well illuminated at any time on a sunny day.

Continuing your drive you will reach Langdon Beck in a further three miles, and if you wish to see Caldron Snout you must keep a sharp lookout for a road on the L which turns off the highway just before the hotel appears ahead at a sharp R-angle bend. Drive along this well surfaced road which rises gradually across the moor to terminate well above the new Cow Green Reservoir. Note however that some distance short of it a narrow side road on the L leads down to Caldron Snout but ends at a locked gate. Since there is room for only one car it is advisable to park the vehicle near the fork. Now walk down the road, pass through the side gate and continue until you reach the top of Caldron Snout which is dominated by the Dam extending across the valley, then scramble down the rocks on its east side to the base of the rapids for the view of them. If you wish to descend on its western side it is advisable to cross the bridge near the top of the fall which is the direction taken by the Pennine Way. On returning to your car, you drive back to the main highway and turn L for the long run over the lofty moors to Alston. And if you propose to explore the country described in the next monograph, you should now make for Appleby by way of the fine road over Gilderdale Forest, which on a clear day reveals the distant Lakeland Fells as a picturesque backdrop to the intervening valley scenery.

Plate 225 **Route 53** — The Tees at Barnard Castle

Plate 226 **Route 53** — Rocky bed of the Tees above Winch Bridge

Plate 227 **Route 53**—A glimpse of High Force

Route 54. This high level walk over the crest of the Pennine chain is for tough trampers only, who will discover it not only unfolds striking scenes of waterplay and desolate moorland grandeur, but also one of the greatest surprises in the hill country of Britain.

If you are staying at the Langdon Beck Hotel you may choose to follow Route 53 to Caldron Snout, whereas if you come from the Youth Hostel nearby you can reach the fall by crossing the Tees for Widdybank Farm and then walk under Falcon Clints. After exploring the rapids, which are most impressive when the stream is in spate, you cross the bridge and follow the cart track to Birkdale. Thence, keep to the path for Moss Shop and continue ahead to Maize Beck where the track rises beside the stream through heather, bent and bog until you attain the lofty plateau. The crest of this watershed is marked by a small cairn on the track, near which stands a pointer to the footbridge you have already crossed; a most useful sign for walkers going in the opposite direction in mist. Here the gentle slopes of Dufton Fell rise on your R and those of Mickle Fell and Murton Fell on your L, but between them you will soon perceive the blue serrated skyline of the Lakeland Peaks far away to the west. You now descend slightly and then the grand metamorphosis in the landscape is suddenly revealed: for High Cup Nick drops away spectacularly at your feet just as if the Titans had gouged out a wild rift in the hillside. The whole of its semi-circular rim is lined with a series of basaltic columns consisting of small buttresses and gullies, with here and there a needle of rock, while the steep slopes below are strewn with scree which varies in size from a tiny pebble to a small cottage. Your track goes to the R and skirts the edge of the precipices, and as you advance there are increasingly broad views of the verdant, patterned Vale of Eden far below. When the rock buttresses merge with the slopes of the moor, you follow a linc of cairns which bear away to the R and guide you to a deserted quarry. On passing through a gate below it you pick up a grassy cart track which meanders down the slopes of Peeping Hill and discloses Dufton Pike away on the R as a conical eminence dominating the village of the same name. You pass through gated pastures, with the lonely farm of Bow Hall on the R, and descend to a lane which leads down to the main road with the village of Dufton on your R.

Plate 228 **Routes 53 and 54**—Caldron Snout and the dominating dam of Cow Green reservoir

Map 24
Cauldron Snout

Red Wing
Beck
Bink Ho.
Greenhills
Pegharn Lo.
Hotel
Wale
53
53
Sand Sike
Widdybank
54
Wheysike Ho.
Fell
54
Cronkley Scar
Caldron Snout
Falcon Clints
River Tees
Cronkley
547m
Skyer Beck
Merrygill Moss
Cronkley Fell
Noon Hill
Merrygill Beck
Long Hurst
Howde
Long Crag
673m

Plate 229 **Routes 53 and 54**—Looking down the Caldron with the rapids in spate

Plate 230 **Routes 53 and 54**—The End of the Rapids

High Cup Nick and Dufton

2,151 feet   656 metres

A convenient centre for the exploration of these two places is Appleby, the county town of Westmorland. It possesses many quaint houses, a castle, a fine church and the famous Moot Hall which occupies a prominent position in the Market Square. Moreover, it stands astride the broad River Eden, whose fishing is said to be good, and is spanned by a splendid bridge giving access to the main highway. A66(T).

Dufton lies in the shadow of the Pennines, some three miles to the north, and is one of the most charming spots hereabouts. Its picturesque cottages, and inn are pleasantly arranged round an oblong green which is cut by the road diagonally and ornamented by a well-executed fountain. High Cup Nick is about four miles due east of the village and the walk up to it is at an easy gradient all the way.

Route 55. Pass under the railway bridge in Appleby and drive to Brampton Tower where the road forks. Take the R branch and continue along the narrow, twisting lane to Dufton where you should park your car and stroll round the village green. Then drive back a short distance until you reach a lane on the L leading to Bow Hall, where you will be well advised to park your car on the grass verge. It is possible to drive a mile or so up the steeper walled cart track, but you may experience some difficulty in turning the vehicle, especially in wet weather when its shoulders are soft and muddy. This gated track rises across the moor, and after it bends away to the R you will soon encounter the last gate into a quarry. Now follow the track which rises round its rim and then go straight ahead following the conspicuous cairns on the higher ground until you sight the gigantic gash of High Cup Nick. Keep to the edge of the precipices until you reach its head, where you may scan its peculiar formation and then enjoy in clear weather the retrospect of the Vale of Eden, backed by the Lakeland Fells.

Plate 104. Route 43. Descends by the stream

Plate 231 The watershed on **Route 54**— High Cup Nick is a few yards away

Skirwith Fell
Rake End
57
Cross Fell
Mine Cottage
or Gregs Hut
Fallow Hill
Kirk Dale
893m
Cross Fell
56
River Tees
Tees Head
56
Swath Beck
Grey Scar
Wildboar Scar
Milburn
Hard Hill
678m
Middle Tongue
Forest
847m
Grumply Hill
Trout Beck
Moss
Iron Howe
Mine
Green Castle
Ore Gill
Knock Fell

Gt Rundale Tarn

Seamore Tarn

Lyt Rundale Tarn

High Cup Nick

Narrow Gate

Beacon

54

689m △

Backstone Edge

55

699m △

High Scald Fell

Peeping Hill

Bluethwaite Hill

Brownber Hill

Sink Beck

Swindale Beck

Dufton Pike
481m △

Town Head

Far Close

Knock

Dufton

Knock Pike
398m △

56

Milburn Grange

HOWGILL CASTLE

Map 25
High Cup Nick, Dufton
and Cross Fell

Plate 232 **Route 55** — Dufton Pike from the village green

Plate 233 **Route 54 and 55**—High Cup Nick

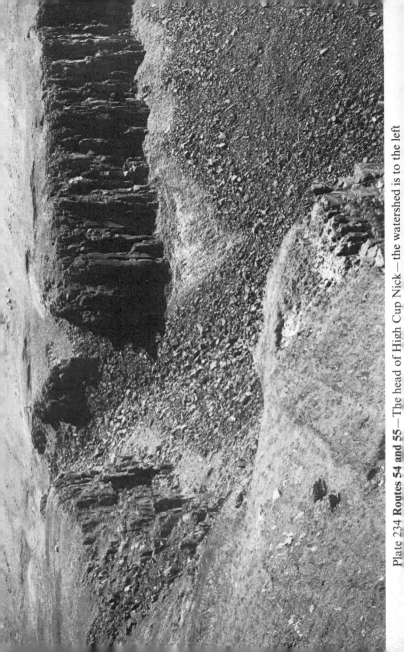

Plate 234 **Routes 54 and 55**— The head of High Cup Nick—the watershed is to the left

Plate 235 **Routes 54 and 55**— The Vale of Eden from the terminal basaltic columns

Cross Fell

Cross Fell	2,930 feet	893 metres
Great Dun Fell	2,780 feet	847 metres
Little Dun Fell	2,761 feet	842 metres

This is the highest peak in the Pennines and stands just inside the Cumbria border where the county boundary between it and Little Dun Fell passes Tees Head, which lies in the col between them. This mountain is really the culminating point in a lofty moorland plateau, and its summit is an almost indistinguishable heap of stones. Its topography thus differs much from the general aspect of the Lakeland Fells, which for stern grandeur are difficult to beat elsewhere in England. To the south-west, Cross Fell is bounded by Kirkland Fell which is rimmed by the crags of Wildboar Scar and then falls more steeply to the patterned fields of the valley, whereas on every other side it is flanked by vast stretches of boggy moorland which are best left alone by the pedestrian. Until the opening of the narrow and steep paved road from Knock to Great Dun Fell, which is surmounted by the conspicuous Radio Station of the Ministry of Aviation, it was customary to ascend this peak from Kirkland which is the nearest hamlet, and from which a disused mine track rises to the old working immediately to the north of its summit, whereas nowadays a car may be driven to a point below the station, whence a walk over the two satellites leads quickly to the cairn.

Route 56. Follow Route 55 to Brampton Tower and take the L fork for Long Marton, then turn R beyond the village for Knock. Here turn L and shortly R for Close Houses, whence continue up the steep and narrow road which as height is gained opens up some fine views of your peak on the L. Observe also the ropeway which at one time connected Milburn Grange with the mine below Great Dun Fell.

Cross Fell

Little Dun Fell

Great Dun Fell

Plate 236 Cross Fell and Satellites from Milburn Grange

Continue your drive until you reach a sharp L turn near a notice board which is about 300 feet below the radio station and park your car nearby. Then walk up the road, and when past the Ministry of Aviation buildings observe your route ahead in which Little Dun Fell stands in a direct line with your peak. Go ahead across the depression and after passing the first eminence descend to the vast quagmire of Tees Head which occupies the whole of the col immediately beneath the scree encircling the flat top of Cross Fell. And here you must pick your way carefully through the drier sections of the bog which, however, do not exist in wet weather. It is therefore safer to keep to the L on the higher and drier edge of the watershed and then make for a grassy break in the scree. On attaining the plateau it is still a long walk due north to the summit cairn which in clear weather opens up a wide panorama to the west in which the Lakeland Peaks form the distant skyline, whereas to the east you look across a wilderness of boggy moorland to the far horizon, which in bad weather is a sinister prospect indeed.

Route 57. follow Route 56 to the fork beyond Long Marton, but take the L branch that goes north to Blencarn, noting on the R the spacious prospect of Cross Fell and its satellites. Turn R in the village for Kirkland and park your car on the grassy verge near the bridge. Keeping the stream on the L, you follow the road through the hamlet which deteriorates after passing the last building on the R, beyond which a gate gives access to the old mine track. This sweeps round to the L and in due course skirts the flanks of High Cap, then bear R past the old pits until you attain the summit slopes to the north-west of Cross Fell. Here you turn R for Crossfell Well, if you can locate it, and then climb the scree to the extensive flat top and cairn on your peak. This ascent covers a distance of about four miles, but if you have a jeep and can obtain permission to drive up the track, you might save a lot of foot slogging.

Great Dun Fell

Plate 237 **Route 56**—The mountain road to Great Dun Fell

Cross Fell | Little Dun Fell

Plate 238 **Route 56**— As seen from Great Dun Fell

Plate 239 **Route 56**—The lonely summit of Cross Fell

Blencathra

Plate 240 **Route 56**—Distant view of the Lakeland fells

Plate 241 Here comes the Helm Wind

Crag Lough and Hadrian's Wall

Known formerly as High Shield Crag, this playground of the rock climber is less than half a mile in length and forms a section of the northern escarpment of Hadrian's Wall. Consisting of igneous rock, it is an excellent example of quartz dolerite and appears as a succession of vertical buttresses, not more than eighty feet high, which are separated by bays riven with gullies. The eastern end of the crag overlooks a blue, reedy lake which is backed by the lonely hills of the Kielder Forest, and to the R reveals the pendent curves of the Roman Wall to Hotbank Crags. The western end of the escarpment is separated from the main crag by a steep break in the cliffs, known as the Appian Way, and on the crest of them both runs the path which is one of the greatest delights of the long walk from Newcastle to Carlisle. Camping is permitted in a grassy hollow at the western terminus of the cliffs, and is only a short step from the Steel Rigg car park which is embowered in trees.

Since Crag Lough is invisible from the Military Road, B6318, which runs parallel with, and to the south of, Hadrian's Wall hereabouts, it is not easily located by the newcomer. The key to its discovery is the famous and now rebuilt Twice Brewed Inn and the nearby Once Brewed Youth Hostel, to the north of which a lane rises to a break in the wall where the Steel Rig car park occupies the centre of a copse. A gate gives access to the path along the Wall and discloses the now prominent escarpment a mile away to the east across the moor; Haltwhistle is conveniently situated for its exploration and is only some three miles distant.

Crag Lough is an excellent climbing ground in dry weather, but like the cliffs of Scafell it faces north and is only illuminated by the sun late on a summer afternoon. A slippery path, choked with vegetation, undulates along the base of the cliffs and is strewn with boulders and scree that have fallen from the face. It is not a place to linger on a cold, wet day.

Map 26
Crag Lough and
Hadrian's Wall

More than sixty climbs festoon the precipices, and those to the west of the Appian Way include the Pinnacle, Impossible and Far West Buttresses. To the east of this break in the cliffs are several others, including Hadrian's Buttress, Jezebel, Tarzan, Central Buttress and Great Chimney. There is also the Girdle Traverse of the Central Buttress which involves nearly 200 feet of very severe climbing. The climbers on Pinnacle Face, illustrated on plate 245, are John Jacobson and Kenneth Wright; they were good enough to make this ascent at my request.

The main cliff shown in plate 246 is a section of the Central Buttress, on whose upper stretches are Y and Crystal Climbs—two very severes. As elsewhere, a number of harder modern routes have been climbed, also. The smaller buttress in the foreground is scaled by a Chimney and Mantelshelf.

Hadrian's Wall extends from Wallsend-on-Tyne to Bowness-on-Solway, a distance of over seventy-three miles. But since it is so well known and as so much literature has already been devoted to it, no detailed description of its splendours is desirable or necessary in a book of this kind. Never-the-less, aside from the excellence of the long tramp from one end to the other, of which the most interesting section lies along the Pennine Way between Thirlwall and Housesteads, it is worth while to make a special visit to the latter. Strong walkers can easily combine it with Crag Lough, as it is located only just over two miles along the wall to the east, or if the walk is undertaken from the car park in the copse the distance there and back is about six miles. Should anyone wish to omit the visit to Crag Lough, there is a spacious car park on the north side of B6318 at New Beggarbog, whence a short walk across the fields leads straight to the well preserved ruins. It should be noted that the highest point on the Roman Wall is at an altitude of 1,230 feet and situated on Winshields Crags which is half a mile west of the Crag Lough car park.

Route 58. Leave your car in the Steel Rigg park and walk eastwards along the crest of Hadrian's Wall, noting the precipitous cliffs of Crag Lough on the L and the lake below. Continue along the Wall to Cuddy Crag which opens up a fine vista of its bends, thence to Housesteads and stroll round the ruins whose original use is indicated clearly by notice boards. The two last photographs require some explanation The granary pillars supported a now vanished floor, and the Roman soldiers would have sat on wooden seats in the latrine over the sewers on either side of the central paved path. They washed their sponges, the equivalent of modern toilet paper, in the water running along the gutter in front of them, and the stone basin at the end was provided for rinsing their hands. This was a wonderful example of ancient hygiene, not equalled until the present century. Then retrace your steps until Crag Lough appears ahead, and after passing Hotbank Farm on the R descend from the Wall and walk back to your car on the north side of the lake, which reveals a comprehensive prospect of the long line of cliffs that look their best on a summer afternoon.

Plate 242 Crag Lough—the long line of cliffs

Plate 243 **Route 58**— Hadrian's Wall approach to Crag Lough, with Milecastle 39 in the foreground

Plate 244 **Route 58**—The Pinnacle from Appian Way

Plate 245 **Route 58**—Climbing Pinnacle Face

Plate 246 **Route 58**—The Crags above the Lough

Plate 247 The ups and downs of Hadrian's Wall—seen from Cuddy Crag

Plate 248 **Route 58**— Ruins of Housesteads

Plate 249 **Route 58**—The Granary at Housesteads

Plate 250 **Route 58**— The Roman latrine at Housesteads

This **route Card** is now in use in Scotland and Snowdonia; the idea is sound and if adopted and used consistently by all climbers and walkers throughout our mountainous country it could be the means of facilitating any call for Mountain Rescue. I hope the English Police will favour its use and distribute the Route Card widely wherever climbers and mountain walkers are lodged. It is, of course, most important that NO DIGRESSION is made from the stated route, otherwise in the event of an accident searchers would be unable to locate the victim.

Let us know
when you go
on our hills

Names and Addresses: Home Address and Local Address	Route
Time and date of departure;	Bad Weather Alternative:
Place of Departure and Registered Number of Vehicle (if any)	
Estimated time of Return:	Walking/Climbing (delete as necessary)

GO UP WELL EQUIPPED - TO COME BACK SAFELY

Please tick items carried:

Emergency Food	Torch	Ice Axe
Waterproof Clothing	Whistle	Crampons
(Colour -	Map	Polybag
Winter Clothing		
(Colour -	Compass	First Aid

Please complete and leave with Police, landlady, warden etc.
Inform landlady or warden to contact Police if you are overdue.

PLEASE REPORT YOUR SAFE RETURN.

Index